Financial Literacy

Literacy
for Teens

D0028846

Chad Foster

Copyright © 2005 by Chad Foster

ALL RIGHTS RESERVED

No part of this book may be reproduced in any form or by any means without the prior written permission of Chad Foster, excepting brief quotes used in connection with reviews written specifically for inclusion in a magazine, newspaper, or electronic review, in which case attribution including www.chadfoster.com is required. Inquiries should be addressed to Rising Books, P.O. Box 1408, Conyers, GA, 30012.

ISBN: 0-9644456-3-8

Printed in the United States of America

First Edition

Cover and Text Design by J.R. Houk
www.jrhouk.com

Contents

Make It

Manage It

Multiply It

Protect It

Final Thoughts

A few people

retire when they are 40.

Most people

work until they hit 67.

Some people

have to work till the day they die.

How about you?

Make It

the Million dollar question

This book is about money – not my money, not your parents' money, but your money. Almost every one of you is going to earn more than $1,000,000 over the course of your life. That's right! More than one million dollars is going to pass through your hands during your career.

From the time you get your first full-time job until the day you retire, you will have to decide what to do with more than a million dollars.

Not possible? No way?

You do the math, and this is not that complicated new math they are teaching in schools these days. I'm talking about basic math – easy to do and simple to understand. Most of you will go to work in your early twenties and then continue working until you retire in your early to mid-sixties. That's just a fact of life. Don't get me wrong; I hope you all retire much earlier than that, but even if you do, the same math applies.

If you get a job earning $30,000 per year when you are in your mid-twenties and then work until you are in your mid-sixties, that's 40 years of work. Even if you never get a raise and make the same $30,000 each year, over the course of your career, you will earn $1,200,000. That's 1.2 million dollars. That's a lot of money – a whole lot.

And just imagine what will happen if you do get a few raises during your career, like almost everybody does. What if you average $40,000 per year instead of $30,000? If you do that, then you will earn 1.6 million dollars during your career.

You see, even with basic math, the numbers don't lie. The chances are real good that, if you are reading this book, you are going to make more than a million dollars during your lifetime.

What will you do with your million dollars?

Have you ever sat at your desk at school and, right in the middle of class, thought to yourself, "What is this all about? Why do I need to learn all this stuff? What does this have to do with my future?" Those are fair questions, and every one of you has a right to ask them. Here's why.

When you walked into your school, you basically made a deal with all of the adults around you – all of the teachers, counselors, principals, and even business people like me. Every one of you pretty much put your future in our hands. You agreed to come to school, sit in class, do your homework, and take your tests. In return for that investment of time, energy, and effort, you deserve more than just a piece of paper that you frame and hang on your wall. You deserve some kind of plan that tells you exactly what you will need to know in order to succeed in the world of work – since that is where you and all of your classmates will eventually end up. The world of work is where you will earn your million dollars.

If we send you out into the real world without the tools you need to succeed, then we have cheated you out of your end of the deal. And that's not fair because you are doing a great deal of work.

Most of you will spend between 10,000 and 15,000 hours in a classroom between first grade and the time you finish your education. That's way too many hours to sit in class and end up with less than *all* the knowledge and skills you need to succeed. We owe you all that knowledge and all those skills in return for the time you are investing in your education.

So what are we going do about it? Well, it seems pretty obvious to me that we owe you a good plan for success. That's not hard to see, but the real question now is, "What should that plan include?" What do you *really* need to know in order to succeed after you spend 15,000 hours in a classroom?

That's an interesting question because the answer to that question is going to change over time. For example, most of you would agree that in order to succeed in today's world, it is very important to have computer skills – at least the basic ones. I totally agree with that statement, but guess what? When I was in school, no one ever taught me anything about computers – nothing! Why not? Why didn't my teachers teach me how to use a computer, how to search the Internet, how to e-mail my friends, or how to use instant messenger?

The answer to those questions is very simple. There were no computers around when I was in school, so learning about computers was not relevant at that time. But today, everybody in school is taught something about computers because it is extremely relevant. It is unbelievably important that we teach every one of you how to operate and work with computers. That is one of the tools young people must have in order to succeed in the real world.

As you can see, the tools we need to succeed today might not be the same tools we needed 10 or 20 years ago or the same tools we will need 10 years from now. That's what makes educating young people like you such a challenge. We can't keep teaching the same old stuff class after class, day after day, month after month, and year after year. We can't stand up in front of you and try to convince you that something is relevant when it's not.

We owe you more than that. We owe you a toolbox that is full of tools that you will need in order to succeed during *your* lifetime, not tools that were needed 50 years ago. Sure, some of the tools needed to succeed 50 years ago will still be needed today, but there are many new skills and a lot of new knowledge that you will need for today's ever-changing world.

The bottom line is this. Everybody eventually finishes school, moves out on their own, gets a job, and makes money. Some people make a little bit of money. Some make a lot of money. Some people make more than they need. Some need a whole lot more than they make. But no matter which group you fall into, nobody wants to lose the money that they work so hard to earn.

What if there were a few things you could learn as teenagers that could prepare you to make, manage, multiply, and protect your hard-earned money? That would be nice, wouldn't it?

On the other hand, what if we let you go all the way through school and never taught you those things? What if we let you sit in a classroom for 15,000 hours and never gave you the tools you need to deal with money? That would be like throwing you out into the middle of the ocean without a life jacket before we taught you how to swim. You deserve better treatment than that.

The bad news is that a lot of people, including me, went all the way through school and never learned much about dealing with money or financial matters. We had to learn by trial and error, and there was usually a lot more error than we would have liked. When we were in school, they forgot to teach us what to do with our money after we earned it. That's the bad news.

The good news is that we aren't going to let that happen to your generation. We can't let that happen to your generation. That's not the deal you made when you walked into school and put your future into our hands.

This book is all about *money* – how to make it, how to manage it, how to multiply it, and how to protect it. If you are investing your time, energy, and effort in an education, you deserve to know this stuff.

This book doesn't have everything you need to know about money, but it's a good start. It won't bore you with a bunch of graphs and charts. The purpose of this book is to make sure that when you start earning money, and maybe you already have, you will understand what you need to know about handling and holding onto that money.

Remember, it's *your* money. I'll see you at the bank.

big bucks & big buckets

If someone told me that I was going to make a million dollars during my career, my first thought would be, "You're nuts!" Then I would ask the obvious question, "How in the world am I going to do that?" That's a fair question and one worth addressing whether you are 12, 15, or 20 years old. In fact, the earlier you start thinking about it, the better off you will be.

This book is all about dealing with money, but before you can deal with money, you have to earn that money. How you earn it will be one of the most important decisions you will ever make. It's not a decision that someone else should make for you, and it's not a decision you should take lightly. Earning money takes up a lot of your time – like eight to ten hours per day for 35 to 40 years of your life. Believe it or not, the average career for most of you will last 86,000 hours.

My only advice to you about earning money is this: make sure you find yourself a job that you enjoy. People who love their jobs tend to be much happier than people who hate their jobs, no matter how much money they make. 86,000 hours is a long time to be miserable!

As soon as you start working, either part-time or full-time, the money will start rolling in. At that point, you will have to begin making lots of decisions about what to do with the money you have left. That might sound a little weird – talking about the money you will have left even before you have spent a single dime of your hard-earned money, but that's the way it works.

Uncle Who?

You are about to be introduced to one of your relatives who will be taking money away from you for the rest of your life. In fact, this relative will usually take some of your money before you ever get your hands on it.

That's right. You will work your tail off to make money, and before you can put it into your pocket or your checking account, one of your relatives – an uncle of all people – is going to snatch some of it away right from under your nose! Not exactly what you'd like to think an uncle would be doing. I mean, when I think of an uncle, I'm thinking birthday presents and holiday gifts, not some guy helping himself to my hard-earned money without even asking if it's O.K. with me.

And you know what's even worse? When this uncle takes his share of your money, he gets to use that money for whatever he chooses. And he doesn't even have to check with you before he spends it.

If this sounds like a rotten deal to you, join the crowd. You have just met an uncle you probably never knew you had. His name is Uncle Sam, a nice name for the United States government, which will be taking income taxes out of your paychecks for the rest of your life. Uncle Sam doesn't call it "taking" your money. He calls it "withholding" payroll taxes. That's probably a good description since Uncle Sam gets his hands on some of your money before you even see your paycheck.

I doubt Uncle Sam will ever be your favorite uncle, and I'm sure he won't be invited to your next family reunion. But he does live forever, and he never stops doing his thing – carving a little cash out of your hard-earned paycheck.

If you have ever worked part-time after school, on weekends, or during the summer, you probably already know the feeling – that there's not much left of your paycheck after taxes are taken out. Most people call what's left after taxes are taken out for Uncle Sam their "take-home pay." That's the amount of money you actually get to take home. And that's the amount of money you have to figure out what to do with.

Think of your Uncle Sam as a guy who shows up on payday at your place of employment with three buckets: one really big bucket for federal income taxes, one medium-sized bucket for Social Security taxes, and a third smaller bucket for Medicare taxes. To make things even worse, in all but seven states, Uncle Sam brings his brother the state government tax collector with him. That guy has a bucket of his own for state income taxes. These guys fill their buckets up with *your* money before you even get your paycheck.

How much does Uncle Sam take? Well, that all depends on how much money you make. There is a 5,000-page tax code that you can read if you have about two years of free time and don't mind being bored to death. But simply put, the more money you make, the higher the tax bracket you will fall into, and the more taxes you will pay. Uncle Sam calls this a "graduated" income tax. Basically, the more you make, the more Uncle Sam will take.

Here's how it works. If you work part-time and make $100 each week, Uncle Sam takes a total of only about 18% out of your paycheck. On the other hand, if you work full-time and earn $40,000 per year, Uncle Sam is going to want about 25% from you ($6,810 for income taxes, $2,480 for Social Security and $580 for Medicare). And if you really do well and earn $100,000 per year, dear Uncle Sam is going to take approximately 30% of your income for a total of $29,646.

Even if you win the lottery, don't think that ten million dollars is all for you. When Uncle Sam and his brother get finished filling their buckets, almost half of your ten million dollars will be gone.

Bucket #1 – Freedom is Not Free

I don't know anyone who enjoys paying income taxes, but taxes are a fact of life. Actually, most taxes are very necessary because they pay for many important services.

Taxes pay for highways and interstates, bridges, buses, and subways. Federal and state income taxes also help pay for public schools, community and technical colleges, and universities as well as the teachers who teach at those institutions. They also help support less fortunate people who lose their jobs or cannot work because of a disability. Income taxes even help pay the salaries of police officers and firefighters who keep us safe.

These are just a few of the many things that Uncle Sam does with the money in his big bucket. But where does the majority of all that federal income tax money go?

We live in one of the greatest countries in the entire world. We are very lucky because we live in a country that believes in freedom – freedom of speech, freedom of religion, freedom to vote, and freedom to watch any television channel you choose. These are all freedoms we enjoy just because we live in the United States. In fact, in the U.S. we have more freedom than anywhere else in the world.

But too many people take their freedom for granted. Freedom comes at a cost, and in some cases it comes at a very high cost. Many young Americans have paid the ultimate price to protect our citizens and to guarantee our freedom. Hundreds of thousands of brave men and women have died in wars as they fought to defend your freedom and mine. These members of the Army, Navy, Air Force, and Marines are all part of the strongest military force in the world, and their job is to protect our nation.

Money from your taxes is used to fund these military forces – to pay for their tanks, planes, guns, bombs, and whatever else they need to protect you and me. Tax dollars are also used to fund the new Department of Homeland Security. Billions and billions of dollars are needed to keep our nation safe and free. Last year alone, Uncle Sam spent $400 billion to pay for our freedom.

Freedom is expensive. Income taxes help pay for freedom.

Bucket #2 – Social In-Security

Some of that money that Uncle Sam snags will be put into bucket #2, called Social Security. The amount of money taken out of your check, before you even get your hands on it, will be listed on your hard-earned paycheck as "FICA" (Federal Insurance Contribution Act) or it might be listed as OASDI (Old-Age, Survivors, and Disability Insurance). Your Social Security taxes are combined with Social Security taxes from millions of other people who work and pay taxes. This money is collected by the government (Uncle Sam) to make sure that when you get too old to work, or if you become disabled and cannot work, you will have enough money to pay for the basic necessities. When someone dies and leaves behind a wife, husband, or children, those family members may also receive Social Security benefits.

The federal government collects all Social Security taxes and is in charge of the whole bucket of Social Security money.

The idea is that the federal government will collect all of that money and then give some of it back to us, a little bit at a time, starting when we are 67 or if we become disabled and cannot work. For some people, this Social Security money will be the only money they have to live on when they retire.

Unfortunately, a lot of people don't save and invest their money while they are still working, so when they finally retire, if they ever get to retire, they don't have enough money to support themselves and their families. These people have to depend on Social Security income to pay all of their bills. This is a horrible situation to find yourself in since Social Security income is not that much money.

In fact, the most you can receive in Social Security income as of now is $1,825 per month, no matter how much Social Security taxes you pay over the course of your career. Even if you pay hundreds of thousands of dollars in Social Security taxes while you are working, the maximum you can get back when you retire is $1,825 per month. Because so many people have to share the Social Security bucket of money – almost 47 million people last year – the average Social Security payment today is $922 per month.

As you can probably see, Social Security income is nice to have, but you will be much better off if you don't depend on Social Security to support your retirement lifestyle. That's why a lot of people don't like this idea of the federal government being in charge of their Social Security taxes. Some people don't think Uncle Sam is doing a very good job of looking after their money. Many people believe that the Social Security pot of money will be empty before they get any of their fair share back from the government.

The same folks who decide how much you're going to pay in income taxes are also the people who are in charge of what will be done with your Social Security taxes. These people who make our laws, those elected to the U.S. Senate and House of Representatives, have a lot of control over what happens to your money.

Fortunately, you and I and all of our friends and family get to decide who serves in the Congress. That's why, as soon as you are 18, you need to vote in every election possible. These people are messing with *your* money, and you should decide who gets to do that.

My advice...don't depend on Uncle Sam to take care of you when you get old.

Bucket #3 – Who Medicares?

When you get old – and I don't mean in your twenties, I mean really old – your body isn't going to work as well as it does today. Lucky for you, this isn't going to happen for quite some time but, eventually, it is going to happen. That, I can assure you! In fact, a friend of mine once told me that the only way to stop getting older is to die right now. I don't recommend that, but I just wanted to make my point.

So the older you get, the more medical problems you will have, the more doctors you will have to see, and the more medicine you will have to take. All of this stuff costs money – lots of money.

Today, as a teenager, you probably go to the doctor that your mom or dad chooses for you. And your doctor bills, as well as the cost of your prescriptions, are probably paid for through your parents' health insurance plan. They might have health insurance through work, buy their own health insurance, or even be on Medicaid.

Eventually, you will be out on your own, making your own money, choosing your own doctors, and even paying your medical bills with your own health insurance. For some of you, this might be sooner rather than later. Whatever you do, don't ever get caught without health insurance. No matter what you have to do, make sure that you always have health insurance. Accidents and illnesses are a fact of life, and they can be the most expensive facts of life you could ever imagine.

One day, when you are about 67, you will stop working and you will lose your health insurance from your job, or you won't have enough health insurance to cover your needs. This is when Uncle Sam steps in to help you out with a discounted health insurance plan.

Medicare is a health insurance program that is funded by some of your income taxes and run by the federal government. You obviously don't need Medicare today, but someday you probably will, and you will be glad it's there when you do. Medicare is mostly for elderly people, but it also covers the medical expenses of people with disabilities who can no longer work.

Medicare is expensive. This year it will cost Uncle Sam almost $250 billion. That's billion with a "b"!

Income taxes help pay for Medicare.

Don't Mess With the I.R.S.

When Uncle Sam shows up on payday and fills his buckets, don't think that your taxes are paid and the party is over. If you make $4,750 or more during the year, you have to file a tax return that explains your income and all the federal and state taxes you have paid. I don't care if you make your money washing cars, flipping burgers, or babysitting. If your total income is $4,750 or more, you owe your old Uncle Sam a tax return. I'm not going to kid you. This is a royal pain in the butt, but everybody has to do it. In fact, there are just a few things that you absolutely have to do to survive in this world. One is breathing, and the other is paying taxes!

Tax returns are due on or before April 15th each year. If you want more information, check it out at www.irs.gov. I.R.S. stands for the Internal Revenue Service, and these guys are the income tax police. They aren't bad people, but they aren't the best people to have knocking at your door. Pay your taxes, and you won't have to worry about the I.R.S.

The whole income tax deal is pretty complicated, but the general idea is pretty simple. The more money you earn, the higher your tax bracket will be, and the more income taxes you will pay. This is good to know because when you start considering any job, you need to know more than just how much the job pays. The real number you need to know is what's going to be left after Uncle Sam and his friends fill up their buckets.

As I mentioned earlier, some people call this their "take-home pay." Others call it "net pay" or "after-tax earnings." Call it whatever you want to call it, but the bottom line is that it is the money you have left to save, to invest, to give away, and to spend.

Remember, we're talking about your money. And what you do with your money is pretty much up to you. But how you handle your money will determine three things:

1. How many years you will have to work before you retire
2. What kind of lifestyle you will have until you retire
3. How much money you will have to live on after you retire

who succeeds?

Money, money, money. People are always talking about money! But, is money a good thing, or is money a bad thing?

Most people would probably say that money is a good thing. I do think money can be a good thing, but sometimes money can actually be a bad thing.

I've had a chance to meet so many incredibly successful people during my life – movie stars, professional athletes, presidents, millionaires, and even billionaires. As you can probably imagine, most of these people have a great deal of money. I have learned from these people that money is not always a good thing and, more important, I have learned that money cannot make you happy. Now, don't get me wrong; there is nothing wrong with money. I happen to like money, but before we get too far into a book about money, it is critical to understand that money cannot and will not make you happy. In fact, I have more miserable rich friends than you can count. This is sad, but true.

When people believe that money will make them happy, money can be a bad thing. Most people who believe this also believe that the more money they have, the happier they will be. This leads to wanting money for the wrong reasons, and when you want money for the wrong reasons, life is miserable.

On the other hand, when you want money for the right reasons, money can be a very good thing. You can do several things with the money you earn, but generally speaking, you have four choices:

1. Spend it
2. Save it
3. Invest it
4. Give it away

DID YOU KNOW?

Teens spend more than $175 billion each year.

...NOW YOU KNOW.

Habits – Good or Bad?

Spending money is not optional. If you want to live, you're going to have to spend money. That's a guarantee. So the question is not *if* you're going to spend money, but rather, *how much* money are you going to spend and *on what* will you spend your money.

Everybody has to make these decisions. Whether you make $6.00 per hour working at a fast food restaurant, or you make $100,000 per year working as a computer programmer, you still have to face the same two questions:

1. How much of your money will you spend?

2. On what will you spend your money?

Obviously, the computer programmer and the burger flipper will probably have different answers, but the questions will always be the same.

When I was a teenager, I made lots of stupid decisions – way too many to describe in a short book like this. Every once in a while, though, I made a really good decision. I made one of those rare *good* decisions when I was about 14 years old. I got a job.

I always worked when I was a kid – part-time after school, sometimes on weekends, and always during the summer. Some of my friends never worked while they were in high school – not even during the summer. I actually liked working. I liked having my own money, and I had a feeling that working as a teenager would pay off later in life. I had no idea why I believed that – I just did.

Well, for me, later in life is now. Over the years I have been blessed with good fortune in several businesses. Through those experiences I've had a chance to meet many successful business people from all over the world.

One day a few years ago, I started thinking about all of those successful people I had met. I was wondering what all the successful people I had met have in common. I was wondering if they all made straight A's in school, or if they all grew up in big cities. I wondered if they all had blue eyes, or if they all had brown hair. I wondered if they all grew up in two-parent families, or if they all had a lot of money when they were kids.

I didn't have to wonder if all the successful people I know are white or if they are all black. They are not all "anything." They are black, white, Hispanic, Asian, and Native American. They are male and female, old and young. They are from big cities and small towns. Some grew up rich, and some grew up poor.

So what do all of these successful people have in common? The answer became very clear as I started to break it down. The successful people I know come from all walks of life, from all backgrounds, and from all cultures. But the common denominator among almost all of these successful people – the one thing that kept popping up every time their stories of success were told – was that *almost every one of the successful people I know worked part-time when they were teenagers.*

They understood at an early age that some day they would be working full-time, and the best way to prepare for full-time work was part-time work. Why? Because it was through those early work experiences that they learned a lot about earning money and what to do with the money that they earned. They also learned how tough it is to earn each and every dollar, so they were careful about how they spent their money.

DID YOU KNOW?

Sam Walton worked part-time as a teenager. He later started a company called Wal-Mart.

Ray Kroc worked part-time as a teenager. He later started a company called McDonald's.

Most successful people worked part-time as teenagers.

...NOW YOU KNOW.

These successful people developed good spending habits when they were young that stayed with them throughout their careers. With spending, as with anything, bad habits are really hard to break.

Manage It

spend control

While some bad habits, like passing gas in public, are totally gross but certainly not life-threatening, bad spending habits can easily destroy you. Bad spending habits don't usually go away as you get older, which is why they call them habits. In fact, bad spending habits usually get worse with age. That's why a lot of people I know make tons of money each year, yet they are just about broke at the end of every year. These people will never be able to retire. They will work until the day they die. Bad spending habits can cause big problems in life.

Why do some people develop bad spending habits? Are they stupid? Are they uneducated? Are they idiots?

No, most people who develop and then continue to have bad spending habits are simply confused. They do not have a grip on the difference between *needs* and *wants*. And people who don't have a clear understanding of the difference between needs and wants usually struggle with financial problems for the rest of their lives.

DID YOU KNOW?

Fact: Smoking cigarettes can cause lung cancer.
Fact: Lung cancer can kill you.
Fact: Most people who start smoking never quit.
Fact: BAD HABITS are hard to break.

...NOW YOU KNOW.

What are your needs? What are your wants? For that matter, what is a need? What is a want?

A need is something that is necessary in your life – something that may be difficult or uncomfortable to live without like food, clothing, or a place to live. On the other hand, a want is something that is not necessary in your life but rather something you would like to have. This is one of the most important concepts that we will address in this book. Young people who understand the difference between needs and wants have a huge head start on the road to financial success.

*"I **need** some new pants to wear to school."*

*"I **want** a pair of $150.00 designer jeans to wear to school."*

Don't get me wrong. Having a few wants in your life is not a problem. Sometimes, wants can be a great motivating factor in accomplishing a goal. The key is not to eliminate wants but rather to keep your wants under control. The danger with wants is that the more we get and the older we get, the more our wants tend to grow. And, as they grow, they also get more and more expensive. That's when the problem gets serious.

*"I **need** transportation to get to work."*

*"I **want** a brand new Lexus SUV to drive to work every day."*

Too many wants can be a dangerous problem that can sneak up on you when you least expect it. People who get confused about wants and needs usually get caught in a vicious cycle. First, they start spending some of their hard-earned money on stuff that they really could live without. Then, as their wants continue to grow, they start spending too much of their hard-earned money on things that are not really necessary. And finally, people whose wants are totally out of control begin to spend money that they don't even have on stuff they definitely can't afford.

This is where it really gets dangerous – more dangerous than you could ever imagine – because people who spend money that they don't have on wants enter a world that almost always spins out of control. It's like playing a game that you have no chance of winning. It's dangerous. It's scary. It can even be deadly!

you've got mail!

An amazing thing is going to happen to you when you reach your late teens. You are suddenly going to have friends that you never even knew you had. They are going to call you and write you, and if you live away from your parents, they might even drop by to see you. When they write and call, they are going to say lots of nice things to you. They will congratulate you for different things and try to make you feel good about yourself.

You may run into these new friends at the mall, at an amusement park, or even at the beach. If you go to college, get ready, because they will definitely be waiting for you there. It will be easy to recognize these friends because they will almost always be giving stuff away — t-shirts, beach towels, CD's — anything to get your attention, anything that will make you cave in, just for a moment.

They will do almost anything to make you believe that they are trying to help you and trying to do something nice for you. Sometimes they will do and say things to you that make you feel like you have won the lottery.

WATCH OUT! These are NOT your friends. These are NOT people who care about you. These are NOT people who want what's best for you. These are people who want you to spend money that you don't have on things you don't need. These are people who want to help you develop bad spending habits.

I promise you, these are not your friends. If they really were your friends, they would call to check on you when you are sick. If they really cared about you, they would drop by to see you after you break up with your boyfriend or girlfriend.

Who are these people? Why are they writing and calling?

If you're 18 or close to it, keep an eye on your mailbox. It will soon be stuffed with letters from all over the country – letters that will make you believe that money grows on trees in your own backyard. What a joke! These people must think you are really dumb.

These letters will be from companies that want to send you a credit card. Most of them won't even know whether or not you have the money to pay for what they hope you will buy with those credit cards. This is where it gets dangerous and scary and, sometimes, even deadly.

Credit card debt is one of the most serious problems that young people face today. I didn't say owning a credit card or even using a credit card is dangerous. I have nothing against credit cards. I have two of them in my wallet right now. In fact, I've had a credit card since I was 17 years old. Having a credit card is not the problem.

The problems with credit cards start when people, too often young people, use those cards to pay for things they cannot afford – meaning they don't have the money to pay for what they are buying, so they charge it to a credit card and think they will pay for it later. For too many young people, "later" never arrives.

Do you know Sean Moyer? Are you sure you don't know him?

When Sean Moyer was in high school, he probably felt like most of you feel. You look forward to the day when you no longer live under your parents' roof, and you no longer have to follow *all* of your parents' rules. That's more than likely true if you are living in a house like the one where I grew up. Almost every time I had a major disagreement with my parents, the whole conflict ended with one of my parents telling me that as long as I lived under their roof, I was going to have to live by their rules. If they said it once, they said it a hundred times, and I never forgot those words. The bottom line was this – whoever owns the house gets to make the rules.

Well, I own my own house now, and so when my parents come to town for a visit, they often stay with me. I always wondered how they would like a taste of their own medicine. So last time they stayed with me, I left them a note to clean all the toilets and showers before they came down for breakfast. They walked into my room with the note and wanted to know if I had lost my mind. I just looked up at them and told them that as long as they were living under my roof, they would have to play by my rules. Guess what they did? Actually, they did nothing. I made that whole story up, but sometimes I wish I had the guts to actually try it!

Back to Sean Moyer... I know you have no idea who Sean Moyer is, but that's not important. Who he is doesn't matter. What happened to him is something you never want to forget.

Sean was a good student when he was in high school – good enough, in fact, to receive a scholarship to the University of Texas at Dallas. So, he packed his bags, moved out of his parents' house in Oklahoma, and headed off to Texas to get an education. The rest of this story is going to make you sick.

Soon after Sean arrived, he ran into some of those "friends" I told you about earlier in this chapter – so-called friends who convinced Sean that he should have his very own credit card. In fact, they eventually persuaded him to sign up for an even dozen. Now we're not talking donuts and eggs here. We're talking credit cards – 12 of those pitiful, painful pieces of plastic! That's right. A bunch of money-hungry salespeople who could care less about Sean Moyer or you or anyone else convinced that poor college freshman that he needed 12 credit cards. They didn't care that Sean only made about $5.00 per hour working at the mall, or that he had no stash of cash in the bank and no rich parents that could bail him out. All they wanted to do was sign him up for as many cards as they could because every card Sean signed up for meant more money in the salesperson's pocket.

Signing up for all those credit cards was Sean's first mistake. Using them was his last mistake. Sean got caught up in a spending frenzy just like many young people do. He bought stuff he didn't need with money he didn't have. For some crazy reason, he kept on using those credit cards until he owed a whopping $10,000. That was $10,000 he didn't have, and it was $10,000 he had no idea how to pay back.

As you can imagine, Sean was scared to death. He felt like a failure. He decided the only way to solve the problem was to move back home to Oklahoma and live with his parents, which he did. He left school and headed home. He even got two jobs to try to pay off his debts, but it just wasn't enough. He couldn't make enough money to get ahead of the payments that needed to be made. The stress was incredible, and he couldn't see any light at the end of this horrible tunnel of credit card debt.

Soon after moving back in with his parents, the pressure and stress from all of his credit card debt finally took its toll on Sean Moyer. He walked into his bedroom one night and hanged himself. His mother found him dead in his closet the next morning.

Sean Moyer is no longer with us because he made a decision to spend money he didn't have on things he didn't need. The real truth, though, is that the $10,000 debt he ran up on his credit cards is *not* what pushed Sean over the edge. If everybody he bought stuff from had told him that he could pay for those purchases over a period of time *without* interest, he might have been able to do it. But, unfortunately, that's not the way it works in the real world of credit cards.

Every time you use a credit card, you are borrowing money from someone who doesn't even know you and who probably doesn't care a whole lot about you. If they did care about you, they would make sure you were able to pay off your debts before they sent a credit card to you in the first place. The sick thing about this whole deal is that credit card companies actually hope you *can't* afford to pay for what you buy with their credit card because that's how they make their money – big money!

It's called double-dipping, and here's how it works. You take your shiny new credit card to the mall, buy a DVD player, and charge it on your credit card. As soon as you sign that credit card receipt, the store has to pay a percentage of the purchase to your credit card company for the privilege of accepting credit cards. That percentage varies, but it's usually two to three percent of the sales price. So the nice guys at the credit card company get their first chunk of cash before you even get out of the mall.

Then they send a bill to you at the end of the month for everything you charged on your credit card that month. They hope you can't afford to pay the bill in full. They even offer to let you pay what they call the "minimum payment." That's all they hope you decide to pay, because if you pay your bill in full, the credit card creeps don't get a chance to rip you off with ridiculous interest rates and finance charges. That's where they hope to make their second chunk of cash – the second dip of double-dipping.

Check this out. Let's say you run up $1,000 on your credit card, buying everything from shoes to DVD's to pizza, and then never charge another dime on that card. Instead of paying off that $1,000 when your credit card bill comes in, you decide to pay only the minimum payment of $20. Big mistake. If you keep doing that, just making the minimum payment month after month, it will take you almost 20 years to pay off that $1,000. Not only that, but over that 20 years you will have paid back the $1,000 you spent *plus* an additional $2,000 in interest (based upon an 18% interest rate). That's the great American rip-off. Don't be weak and get caught in this rip-off. If you do fall into this trap, you could still be paying for that stupid pizza you bought with your credit card 20 years after you ate the last slice of pepperoni and cheese.

Just as important, don't be fooled by companies that promise super-low interest rates or even "no interest" for a few months. That's another trap, just bait to hook you so they can reel you and your hard-earned cash in at a later date. As you go through life, some things will seem too good to be true – like "no interest" for six months on a credit card. Usually, when something seems too good to be true, it's probably *not* a good deal for you in the long run.

The bottom line is this: don't ever sign up for a credit card unless you are prepared to and are capable of paying off the total balance at the end of every month – not most of the balance, but every dime of the balance, and not most of the months, but every month.

Credit card companies hate it when young people pay off their total balance every month. Why? It's simple. When you pay the total balance every time you get your monthly statement, you are basically borrowing money from the credit card company for free. That's right. You don't pay one penny for the convenience of using a credit card. No interest, no fees, and no getting ripped off.

Don't spend money that you don't have on credit card purchases, even if all your friends are doing it, and, yes, even if your parents are doing it. Just because they are your parents does not mean that you have to make the same stupid mistakes that they make! When those credit card salespeople come knocking at your door, ask them if they have ever heard of Sean Moyer, the kid who hanged himself in his closet.

The time will come when it might make good sense for you to have a credit card. If you need to make a big purchase, a credit card can protect you from having to carry around too much cash. Most important, when you do use a credit card and then pay your bill on time (every time!), you will be establishing a good credit record which will help you later on when you want to rent an apartment or buy a car.

It works both ways, though. Good credit will help you when you get out on your own. Bad credit will make your life miserable. You only have to mess up a couple of times – pay a bill late or write a bad check – and the world will never let you forget it.

Your credit report is like a report card that never goes away. And your credit rating is a lot like your reputation. It's tough to survive with a bad one, but life can be pretty sweet with a good one.

Multiply It

bank some bucks

Of the four things you can do with your money – spend, save, invest, and give away – spending money is the only thing that you cannot avoid, unless, of course, you live in a cardboard box, don't wear clothes, and starve yourself. Spending is pretty much a sure thing. And since spending is a given, it probably should have been last on the list instead of first, because how much of your money you spend should be based on what you have left after you save, invest, and give away some of your hard-earned cash.

Saving should be listed way ahead of spending since it is one of the best habits you can develop in the financial world. It's called "paying yourself first," because saving is a form of rewarding yourself over time. If you learn to save while you are a teenager, then there is a really good chance you will be able to avoid money problems for the rest of your life.

Speaking of saving, I heard a great story recently about a lady who worked as a waitress at the same restaurant, Jessie's Diner, for 40 years. This lady always walked to work, didn't seem to buy a lot of new clothes, and usually ate her meals at the diner before and after work. She loved her job and had tons of regular customers. She got paid in tips, so nobody really knew exactly how much money she was making. She almost never missed work, and once a week she would stop by the bank on her way home.

This lady always had a smile on her face. She had tons of friends who came to see her at work, and they all hung out together on weekends. Everybody called this lady "Doodles" because she was always scribbling little doodles and numbers on paper napkins at work. She would write a bunch of numbers on the napkins and then fold them up and stick them into her pocket. Nobody, except Doodles, ever knew what was written on those napkins.

After 40 years Doodles decided it was time to call it quits, so she told the manager at Jessie's Diner that she was going to retire and buy a house at the beach.

Needless to say, the restaurant staff, her customers, and all of her friends were sad to hear that she would be leaving, so they all got together and threw a huge going-away party for Doodles. When the party was over, she gathered up all of her stuff and started to walk out of the diner one last time. As she passed the table closest to the exit door of the restaurant, Doodles reached over and grabbed a paper napkin from the table. She sat down for a minute, just like she had done every day for 40 years, and scribbled some numbers on the napkin. Doodles had a routine, and even on her last day, after 40 years, she was sticking to that routine. Doodles walked out of Jessie's Diner and went straight to the bank across the street, just like she always did.

The bank manager met Doodles at the front door of the bank and told her he had heard the news about her retirement and her plans to move to the beach. Mr. "Know-it-all" banker was wondering to himself how this little old lady was ever going to be able to afford to buy a house at the beach. He knew Doodles had been a waitress at Jessie's Diner for most of her life, and he was sure that a waitress could not possibly have earned enough money to buy a house at the beach. She probably has no idea how much a house at the beach would cost, he thought.

Doodles explained to the bank manager that she was going to have to close all of her accounts at the bank so she could open new ones closer to her home at the beach. The banker said, "No problem," and then he asked Doodles for her account numbers so he could look up all of the accounts and write her a check for the total. She pulled a crumpled up paper napkin out of her pocket and handed it to the bank manager.

"Here are all of my account numbers and the total value of all of my accounts," said Doodles. The manager took the napkin from her and copied the account numbers, but he never looked at the dollar amount Doodles had listed as the total of her account balances. After he typed her account numbers into the computer, Mr. "Know-it-all" banker handed the napkin back to Doodles. He was actually surprised to see that Doodles had more than one account.

All of a sudden, the bank manager's eyes popped wide open as he stared in disbelief at the computer screen.

"Is everything okay?" asked Doodles.

"There must be some kind of mistake," the banker barked from behind the computer desk. "Are you sure these account numbers are correct?"

"Yes sir," answered Doodles.

The banker asked Doodles one more time if she was absolutely, positively sure that she had given him the right account numbers.

Doodles did her best to remain cool, and with a slight grin on her face, she stated very politely that she had been banking at this bank for 40 years so she knew the account numbers like the back of her hand.

"There must be some mistake. This can't be possible," the bank manager snapped as he looked back at the computer screen. Then he asked Doodles about the other number on her crumpled-up napkin.

Doodles explained that the other number on the napkin was the total dollar value of all her accounts. For 40 years she had stopped by the bank every week to check her account balances and write the total on a paper napkin. That way, she always knew how much money she had.

"That's why I'm sure there is some kind of mix-up here," continued Mr. "Know-it-all" banker. I think there must be a glitch in the system because this crazy computer is telling me that you have a total of $1,839,486.35 in your accounts, and I know that can't be right."

While the bank manager was still talking, Doodles pulled the wrinkled napkin out of her pocket and checked the number written right under her bank account numbers.

"Actually, that number is correct. That's exactly what I have written on my napkin. As of today, my accounts should be worth $1,839,486.35," she said with a smile as she showed the bank manager the napkin.

"How can that be possible?" explained the bank manager. "You have been a waitress at a dumpy little diner for the past 40 years. I know you couldn't have made that kind of money there."

"Maybe not," admitted Doodles, "but what money I did make, I saved most of it and let it earn more money in CD's, savings accounts, and an IRA over the past 40 years.

I never took any money out of this bank for 40 years, and it has slowly but surely grown to be worth almost 2 million dollars," she explained. Then she politely asked the bank manager to close all of her accounts and write her a check for $1,839,486.35.

The frustrated bank manager closed all of Doodles' accounts and proceeded to write the biggest check he had ever written for a lady he had least expected to be one of the wealthiest customers at his bank.

Doodles finally got her check, and just as she was walking out the door, she turned around and said to the banker, "Oh, and by the way, if you ever find yourself down at the beach, please be sure to stop by and say hello!"

Saving is a really good habit. Doodles had been saving her money, week after week, for 40 years.

Most people who end up with a lot of money didn't make a whole bunch of money over a short period of time. Most of them made decent money over a long period of time, but somehow, somewhere, they learned the importance and power of saving money.

There are lots of good reasons to save money. Here are a couple of them.

(1) Rainy Days − In the real world of weather, the sun doesn't shine every day. Some days you wake up and it's cloudy outside, some days it rains, and some days a storm moves in, and it really pours. That's the way it is in the real world of money, too. Just as soon as you think everything is O.K., and you have your finances under control − BAM! A financial storm hits, and you need money *now*. It happens to all of us. Maybe your car breaks down, and the guy wants $600 to fix the problem. You either pay the $600 or live without a car. This month it's the car. Next month it's something else.

43

It's not a matter of *if* it's going to happen; it's simply a matter of *when*. Financial storms will hit you; that, I promise. The secret is to have money before you need it and never get caught needing money before you have it.

DID YOU KNOW?

Teenagers today spend 98% of the money they earn.

...NOW YOU KNOW.

(2) Major Purchases – We all have to make major purchases during our lives – things like televisions, cars, vacations, and computers. Those purchases almost always seem to cost more than we thought they would. As you already know, I think paying for these major purchases with credit cards is the worst idea in the world, unless you pay the whole bill at the end of every month. These major purchases are the things you need to be saving your money for, so you'll have the money when you need it, and you won't have to borrow it.

The good news is that saving money for most major purchases is actually pretty easy. A little here and a little there adds up very quickly.

I used to come home every day and dump all my spare change into an empty milk jug on the floor of my closet. Some days it was a pocket full of nickels and dimes. Other days, it was just a few quarters. But I did it every day for a couple of years. When the jug was full, I decided to count it to see how much money I had. At the last minute, though, I was too lazy to count it, and since I didn't think it was all that much money anyway, I just dropped it off at our church. The church called the next week to thank me for the generous donation. I was sure they had my little donation confused with a donation from someone else, until the guy from the church told me that the change in my old milk jug had added up to almost $400. I couldn't believe it. A nickel here, a quarter there, and before I knew it, that stupid jug had four hundred bucks in it.

Some habits are bad. Some habits are good. Saving money is one of the good ones.

make money while you sleep

When I was 18, I took some time off from school and drove across America. Every day, I drove three hours and then stopped for the night, wherever I happened to be. Sometimes I stopped in small towns, and sometimes I spent the night in larger cities. I started in Louisiana and headed west, trying to make as many stops as possible in towns where I knew somebody – but not just anybody. It had to be someone who had an extra bed or sofa and someone who didn't mind if I crashed at their place for the night. When I had to stay in a hotel, I stayed in the cheapest one I could find. I had saved up some money for this trip, but I didn't want to blow it all, so I watched every dime I spent.

If you head west from Louisiana, the next state is Texas, which is huge. It takes 16 hours to drive from one side of Texas to the other, so I had to make five stops as I made my way across the state. One of the stops I made was in Midland, which isn't a great big city, but it isn't exactly a small town, either. I made a stop in Midland for one reason; my dad had a friend there, and his friend was nice enough to let me stay at his house for the night. That meant I didn't have to blow any cash on a hotel, and maybe I'd even get a free dinner out of the deal.

Actually, I got a lot more than a free room and a meal. On that night I spent in Midland, I got some of the best advice I have ever gotten from anyone, anywhere. I spent the night at Mr. George Conly's house. Mr. Conly is my dad's friend, and he also happens to be an extremely successful businessman.

While I was in Midland, Mr. Conly never talked about his own money, which I thought was pretty cool, but at dinner that night, he did ask me about *my* money. Well, not exactly my money, because he knew I didn't have very much money since I was just 18 years old. But Mr. Conly taught me something about money that night that I will never forget.

Right before we finished dinner, Mr. Conly looked at me and asked me what I wanted to do when I got out of school. A lot of adults ask kids that question. Sometimes I wonder if they really care about the answer, or if it's just the first thing that comes to their minds when they have to have a conversation with a younger person. Mr. Conly asked me that question because he wanted to make a point – a very important point.

I told him that when I finished school, I wanted to be a professional tennis player. That had been my dream for several years. In fact, I had been pursuing that dream non-stop for quite some time, so I told Mr. Conly all about my goals and how I planned to achieve my dream.

Even though Mr. Conly listened very closely to my answer, it really didn't matter what my answer was. He had only asked the question to teach me an incredibly valuable lesson. As soon as I finished telling Mr. Conly about my plans to be a professional tennis player, he looked up at me and said, "That's great, but it really doesn't matter."

At first I thought he was really being rude. I mean, what kind of person tells an 18-year-old kid that his dream doesn't matter? In this case, it was a very wise person, and I will always remember the advice that he gave me that night.

I was pretty hard-headed when I was a teenager. Actually, I was really hard-headed and, most of the time, pretty darn stubborn. But luckily for me, I learned at an early age that when I was in the company of a successful person, the best thing for me to do was to close my mouth and open my ears. You can learn some of the greatest secrets to success by listening instead of talking.

That night in Midland, Texas, I learned something about money that changed my life, and it will change yours, too. It doesn't matter who you are, where you live, how big your house is, or how much money your parents have; Mr. Conly's advice is for you.

Mr. Conly told me that it really didn't matter what career I chose after I finished school, because the bottom line would be the same.

He said, "Chad, if you don't make money while you sleep, you will never really get ahead financially."

Right when he said it, I was thinking, "What in the world is this guy talking about?" Then he explained. He said that it doesn't matter what your job is – whether you're a doctor, a plumber, a teacher, or a professional football player. You can only earn as much money as there are hours in the day. If you are a plumber, and you get paid by the hour, you can only work so many hours each day, which means there is a limit to how much money you can make. By the same token, even if you are a doctor, you can only work so many hours each day, and so you, too, are limited as to how much money you can make. The doctor might make more than the plumber, but both can only earn a limited amount of money.

So what does it mean to make money while you sleep? And why was Mr. Conly so determined to get the message across to me? Making money while you sleep means just what it says. Literally, you can make money while you are totally asleep.

The money you make at your job day after day, week after week, is called *earned* income – meaning that you worked for that money, or you earned it. The money you make while you sleep is considered *unearned* income because it is not money you worked day after day to make.

Mr. Conly's advice was this: if you really want to get ahead, you have to learn how to invest money when you are young and then get into the habit of investing, even if you don't earn a lot of money.

The secret to investing is to let your money earn more money for you. That way, when you are ready to retire, you will have all the money that you earned for yourself *plus* all of the money that your money earned for you.

The first page of this book refers to some people who retire at age 40, some who work until they are 67, and some who have to work until the day they die. People who have enough money to retire at an early age are people who learn how to make money while they sleep.

I could bore you to death with a whole bunch of charts and graphs on investing, but I promised not to do that, and I'm not going to break that promise. But I do have some advice.

You can read all there is to read about investing – newspapers, books, magazines – and even check out some of the investing shows on TV, but the best place in the world to learn about investing is from people you meet who have been investing for a while. These people have "been there – done that," and most of them will be more than happy to share what they know with you. They will tell you how important it is to invest in different types of things – it's called *diversifying* your investments – and the really successful investors understand how to do this. They will also tell you that investments that work today might not be the best investments a few years from now. They will explain to you that it is important to be flexible when investing.

You can invest in all kinds of stuff – stocks, bonds, real estate, businesses, and more. Most importantly, you have to decide what's best for you. The only way to know what's best for you is to do your homework and research your investments. The secret is to start investing when you are young and make it a habit, so your money will have more time to make more money for you.

I'm not here to tell you how to invest your money, but here's a short story that might interest you. I have a friend, Rachel, who just started high school last year. Rachel works part-time after school and on weekends, so she always has some extra cash to spend on stuff she wants as well as stuff she needs.

The only problem is that at the end of almost every week, Rachel has empty pockets, meaning she's broke because she has spent all of her cash. Rachel works hard for her money, and it's none of my business what she does with it, but I hate to see anyone work that hard only to find herself out of cash at the end of every week.

Just for the heck of it, I stuck my nose in Rachel's business a few weeks ago and asked her where all of her money was going. Turns out, a lot of her cash was going right down her throat and into her stomach. Rachel was buying two soft drinks every day at school, spending $2.00 per day on the stuff. Then, on Saturdays, she was doing the same thing, so over the course of the week, she was dumping $12.00 worth of soft drinks into her stomach.

That means every month, almost $50.00 was flying out of Rachel's pocket into a vending machine.

Don't get me wrong, there's nothing wrong with downing a Coke or a Mountain Dew every once in a while. I do it myself on occasion. But what would happen if Rachel made a brilliant decision to give up the soft drinks and take that same fifty bucks that she had been spending each month on soft drinks and, instead, invested that money?

Here's what could happen. Rachel, or you or anyone else, could invest $50.00 a month starting when she is a teenager and continue doing that every month for 15 years. Then, even if she stopped investing $50.00 each month and just let her investments continue to grow, you'll never believe how much money Rachel could easily have when she is ready to retire 36 years later. This is going to blow you away, so get ready. If you invest $50.00 per month for 15 years, starting now, and then leave it invested for an additional 36 years, you could very well have $675,000 when it's time to retire (based on earning 10% annually on your investments)!

So, if my friend Rachel would be willing to give up her soft drinks and dump that $50.00 per month into investments, instead of into her stomach, she could be sitting on $675,000 when she retires. It's hard to believe, but it's true, and you can do the same thing.

Rachel is a perfect example of making money while you sleep. Investing, like saving, is a journey. It's usually a pretty long journey, but like a lot of long journeys, it's usually well worth the trouble. It's important to remember that most investments carry risk with them, which means that there are no guarantees, and sometimes you won't make the money that you hoped you would make. Over the long haul, though, wise investing has proven to be the best way to reach your financial goals.

People who start saving when they are young and young people who learn how to make money while they sleep end up in great financial shape at an early age, but they don't get there overnight. Financial success is a process. It takes time. It takes focus. It takes dedication, and it takes discipline.

Some people have a hard time putting time, focus, dedication, and discipline together in an effort to accomplish something they want very badly. In fact, most people just can't do it, and that's why most people never reach their financial goals.

Mountain Top

Why do some people fail while others succeed?

I believe most people who fail at investing fail because they want to take the whole journey in one giant step. That kind of thinking is called instant gratification, but, unfortunately, investing doesn't work that way. Investing is like climbing a mountain; it's risky, you have to take it one step at a time, and the sooner you start, the sooner you will get to the top.

Just ask my friend Erik Weihenmayer. He knows a little bit about climbing mountains. Erik is one of those guys who loves to do extreme activities. He has lots of hobbies, but his real passion is climbing mountains – really tall mountains.

Last year, I had dinner with Erik in Atlanta, and he was telling me about one of his mountain-climbing adventures. He had just returned from an amazing journey where he successfully climbed to the top of Mt. Everest – the tallest mountain in the world at 29,029 feet. If you want to know how high that is, just look up in the sky one day when an airplane is flying over. If the plane is so small that you can barely see it, take another look. That plane is probably flying approximately 30,000 feet up in the air. That's how tall Mt. Everest is, and my friend Erik Weihenmayer climbed all the way to the top.

Erik and his nine fellow climbers faced incredible danger along the way and dealt with unbelievable challenges every day. The journey to the top of Mt. Everest took several weeks, and the temperatures were way below zero most of the time. Each day seemed to bring another life-threatening experience – frostbite, hurricane-force winds, icy slopes, and deep crevices. Most people who attempt to climb the tallest mountain in the world give up and turn back before they get to the top. Climbing Mt. Everest is so dangerous that some climbers who try to conquer the mountain even end up dying along the way. People who attempt to climb Mt. Everest are willing to risk it all, even their lives, for the reward of reaching the peak of the tallest mountain in the world.

At dinner that night, Erik impressed upon me the importance of taking this journey one day at a time, one hour at a time, and in some cases, one step at a time.

"One day at a time" is exactly what it takes to be successful with investing. You may even have to take it one step at a time, but you can start with a little and end up with a lot. It's just like climbing a mountain. The sooner you start, the sooner you will be making your way to the top of your financial mountain. And remember, getting to the top is your goal, but it is critically important to enjoy the journey along the way. The best way to do that is to start investing early in life, do your homework, understand the risks, and not be greedy. There is an old saying that successful investors live by: "Pigs get fat and hogs get slaughtered." The point is that smart investors know when to take their profits and consider other investments. That's how their bank accounts get "fat" like the pigs. On the other hand, people who get greedy and want to make too much money in too short a time span often get slaughtered, just like the hogs!

Ninety-nine percent of wealthy people did not get there in one day or on one financial deal. Just about everybody I know who has made a great deal of money has made it gradually, over an extended period of time...kind of like climbing the tallest mountain in the world.

Why is Erik Weihenmayer's story so amazing?

Erik climbed 29,029 feet to the top of Mt. Everest. You might think, "So what? Who cares? Other people have climbed 29,029 feet to the top of Mt. Everest."

That's true. But those other people weren't *blind* like Erik Weihenmayer. That's right; my friend Erik Weihenmayer is totally blind, and he has been for 20 years.

Why do some people succeed while others fail?

Start investing early in life. Start with just a few dollars – but, most of all, *just start*, and take it one step at a time. Remember Mr. Conly's great advice. Make money while you sleep!

you can't take it with you

After you spend some of your money, save some of your money, and invest some of your money, what do you do with the money that's left? Maybe that's a stupid question, because maybe there's nothing left after you spend, save, and invest your hard-earned cash. That's why the order of the list is the most important part of it. If your list is in the wrong order, then financial success will be hard to achieve.

I know a man who started working part-time when he was eight years old. He says it taught him a lot about how to make, manage, and multiply his money. This man's name is Mr. "C." It really doesn't matter what his real name is, but I might tell you later, anyway.

When he got out of school, Mr. C opened a tiny little restaurant in a small town in Georgia. He worked hard at that business, and the business grew quickly. Before long, he had two restaurants, then four, and then ten, until today, when Mr. C now has more than 1,100 restaurants scattered all over the United States. They sell chicken at Mr. C's restaurants, and sales at the average restaurant are more than $1,000,000 each year. That means total sales at all of Mr. C's restaurants are more than one and a half billion dollars every year – not just one year, but every year – year, after year, after year.

That's so much money that it's ridiculous. Just think, if you divide 1.5 billion dollars by the number of days that Mr. C's restaurants are open each year, you would figure out that each day, Mr. C's company earns more than $4,800,000. That's almost 5 million dollars, every single day!

If you think that's a lot of money, check this out. If Mr. C wanted to, he could snap his fingers and make $250 million more every year, just like that. If he decided to do that, his company sales would increase from 1.5 billion dollars to more than 1.7 billion dollars every year.

What would you do if you could snap your fingers, and your company would make an extra $250 million each and every year?

The answer to that question probably seems pretty obvious, unless you are Mr. C. It is true that Mr. C could make one simple decision, and, immediately, his company would generate $250 million more every year. Yes, Mr. C could do that, but he won't.

Why won't he do that? Is Mr. C crazy?

No, I don't think he's crazy. I actually talked to him on the phone the other day, and he didn't sound crazy to me. Mr. C is just different from most people. He has the same four choices we all have with the money we earn – spend, save, invest, and give away. But most of us have the list of choices in the wrong order. Mr. C has his list in the perfect order:

1. Give away
2. Save
3. Invest
4. Spend

Mr. C's real name is Truett Cathy, and he is the founder of a chain of restaurants called Chick-fil-A. Mr. Cathy made a decision when he opened his first restaurant, 58 years ago, that he would never be open on Sundays. He believes his employees should spend one day a week with their families, and Sunday is the day he chose. So every Chick-fil-A in America – all 1,100 plus restaurants – is closed on Sundays.

As I said earlier, Mr. Cathy could decide tomorrow to start opening his restaurants on Sunday. If he did that, his company's sales would increase by almost 250 million dollars each and every year. That will never happen because Mr. Cathy is willing to give up that $250 million every year just so his employees – all 35,500 of them – can spend Sundays with their families.

Mr. Cathy has his financial list in the right order. With the millions of dollars that come his way from Chick-fil-A, he always keeps his list in the same order. First, he gives some of his money away. Then he saves some of the money. Next, he invests part of this money. And last, always last, he spends some of his money.

GIVE, SAVE, INVEST, and SPEND. If you can stick with that order, you will be financially successful almost every time.

DID YOU KNOW?

Americans are the most generous people on the earth. Last year, they gave more than $180 billion to charities.

...NOW YOU KNOW.

Whatever you do, don't read this story about Truett Cathy and think that it's no big deal to give up 250 million dollars a year when your company's revenues are 1.5 billion dollars each year. Mr. Cathy didn't start closing his restaurants on Sundays and giving up all that money *after*

59

his company was a huge success. That would have been the easy thing to do, but that's not what Mr. Cathy did. Chick-fil-A restaurants have never been open on Sundays, even when Mr. Cathy was almost broke and trying to get his very first restaurant up and running. That's right – before Mr. Cathy ever made dollar number one off of his company, he decided to give up a lot of what he could have earned.

Today, Mr. Cathy not only gives up 250 million dollars each year, but he also gives the money needed to operate foster homes for 120 foster children, funds a summer camp that has hosted 21,000 children, and has provided college scholarships for more than 16,500 students.

Giving is not easy. It's not the natural thing to do for most people, especially people who don't have a lot of money. But, in my opinion, if giving were easy, it wouldn't be important. The average person doesn't understand the importance of giving at an early age. Don't be average.

It's probably a little weird thinking about giving some of your money away when you're just a teenager. But giving is a habit, a good one, that needs to be developed at an early age. Maybe you can only give away a few dollars here and there right now. That's fine, because how much you give is not what's important. The important thing is that you get into the habit of giving.

No matter who you are and no matter where you live, there is always somebody else in this world who has less than you have. Get into the habit of giving away some of your money. A great way to get into this habit is to make a decision right now to set aside a certain percentage of what you earn to give away to someone or to some organization that helps others who are less fortunate. It could be 5%, 10%, 20%, or even more, but make a commitment to give that percentage away every time you earn some money. If you put giving at the top of your list, like Mr. Cathy does, you will never have to worry about whether or not the money will be there to give away.

Whether you are 16 or 60, and whether you give $10.00 or $10,000, there are three things that I can promise you.

1. It always feels good to give.
2. It helps others when you give.
3. Giving is the right thing to do.

Protect It

time, gas, & money

What do time, gas, and money have in common? Somewhere in the next few pages, I hope I can answer that question.

When you wake up each morning, regardless of what time that might be, one thing is certain: there is only so much time left in your day. If you get up at 7:00 a.m. and then go to sleep at 10:00 p.m. that night, you will have 15 hours to do whatever it is you need to do that day. Obviously, if you sleep until noon and go to bed at midnight, your day will last only 12 hours, and your parents might be a little ticked off. In any case, there are only so many hours in each day, 24 to be exact, and "an hour is an hour," any way you look at it. It's 60 minutes, and no matter what you do, you can't jam more than 60 minutes into one hour.

That means in order to get everything done that you need to get done, you are going to have to do something that a lot of people have a hard time doing – manage **time**.

Many people, young and old, get into trouble day after day because they don't allow enough time to do the things that they must get done, and they spend too much time doing other things that aren't as important. So, they run out of time - all the time. These people are late for some appointments and don't show up for others; they constantly run around like chickens with their heads cut off because they are always short on time. I know people like that. You know people like that. They drive you nuts because they are always late, always in a hurry, and always stressed out.

That's no way to live, and it's easy to avoid. All you have to do every day when you wake up is make a short list of the things that you need to get done that day and decide how long it's going to take you to do each thing on the list. It's pretty simple. When you are making the list, if it doesn't look like you are going to have enough time to accomplish some of the stuff, then, right then and there, you adjust the list to be sure you have enough time to get it all done. You don't try to make the change in the middle of the day after you're already late, out of time, or totally stressed out.

It's called time management, and people who can manage their time are always more successful than people who can't. There is a limited amount of time in each day, 24 hours, whether you live in California, Texas, or Hong Kong. You don't want to run out of time any more than you want to run out of... **gas**.

Suppose you are able to buy only a certain amount of gas for your car each week. Whatever the amount is, you want it to last the entire week. If you use too much of your gas the first few days of the week, you won't have enough gas to go to the places you need to go at the end of the week. Even worse, you might be on your way to work on the last day of the week when, out of nowhere, you hear your engine sputter, and it feels like your accelerator isn't working because, guess what! You are running out of gas. It is a horrible feeling. Trust me, I've done it.

Not making it to your destination is bad enough, but the frustration and embarrassment of running out of gas on the side of the road is a hundred times worse, not to mention that, depending on where you run out of gas, it can be downright dangerous.

Remember, with time, it's called "time management." In a very similar way, with gas, it's called "fuel management." If you ever watch one of those auto races on TV, you will hear them talk a lot about fuel management. If the race car drivers and their pit crews do not manage their fuel properly, they could be about to win a big race and all of the money that goes with such a big win, but instead, they run out of fuel on the last lap and blow the whole race.

If you don't think fuel management is all that important, then I dare you to get on an airplane with a pilot who doesn't understand how to manage the plane's fuel.

There's nothing worse than running out of gas unless, of course, you run out of... **money**.

Nobody wants to run out of money. The really bad news is that many people do run out of money – month, after month, after month. And it's not just people who make small amounts of money who run out of cash again and again. Believe it or not, lots of people who make big bucks run out of money all the time.

That's why time, gas, and money have a lot in common. If you can't manage your time, you don't get stuff done. You always run late, and you are constantly stressed out. If you don't understand fuel management, you run out of gas on a dark country road, and some creep pulls over and robs you. Likewise, if you don't know how to manage money, all of your cash is gone before the next paycheck arrives, and life gets really rough.

DID YOU KNOW?

Most lottery winners spend all of their winnings and are broke within five years.

...NOW YOU KNOW.

Some people call it money management, but most people call it a budget. When I was a kid, I hated the word "budget" because every time I heard that word, it was used in a sentence to tell me I couldn't have something I wanted (and thought I needed). Almost all parents use the word on a regular basis – "We can't buy this or that for you because we're on a budget" or "We can't go there on vacation because we're on a budget." No wonder most of us grow up and can't stand the word "budget." For most of us, when we were young, the word "budget" meant, "Can't have, can't do, can't buy, can't go."

There's nothing wrong with feeling that way when you're a kid, but the day you earn your first dollar, your opinion of the word "budget" should change.

"Budget" is actually a very good word. You can make $100,000 a year and still be on a budget. It might not be the same budget you were on when you made $30,000 a year or just $6.00 an hour, but it's still a budget. A budget is simply a plan that says here's how much money I earn after taxes each month, and here's how I am going to give away, save, invest, and spend that money. People who set up a budget for themselves and stick to it almost never run out of money before their next paycheck arrives. And people who live on a budget almost always get to retire earlier than people who don't understand budgets. Having a budget at the beginning of the month keeps you from scrambling to get out of trouble at the end of the month.

A budget helps you establish your limits. It tells you what you *can* afford and gives you a roadmap for achieving your financial goals – no matter how large or small they might be. The bottom line is simple: if you try to live without a budget, financial success is a long shot. With a budget, it's more like a slam-dunk.

Keep in mind: if you can't manage a little bit of money when you're young, you'll never be able to manage a lot of money when you get older.

Remember these three things about budgets:

1. Budgets are for everyone, no matter how much or how little money you earn, and no matter how young or how old you are.

2. The sooner you get into the habit of living on a budget, the more financially successful you will be.

3. "Budget" is not a bad word. It's a really good word.

the $100,000 mistake

Your budget not only tells you how much you can spend each month, but even more importantly, it tells you how to prioritize your spending. If your spending priorities are messed up, you can be earning big bucks and still find yourself in big trouble financially.

Making money is a good thing. Managing and multiplying moncy is even better, but making, managing, and multiplying money are all a great big fat waste of time if you don't know how to *protect* your money.

How are you supposed to protect your money?

Some people don't think they need to worry about protecting their money until they have a ton of cash. Some people aren't very smart. Even some really bright people aren't very smart when it comes to protecting their money. It's a horrible thing to see people who work their butts off to make good money, but then lose it all because they are clueless about how to protect it.

Protecting money is all about being prepared for the unexpected, avoiding disaster when the unexpected happens, and reducing your risk of losing everything you have.

That's why protecting your money should be a no-brainer. And that's why the first dollars you set aside to spend in your budget *must* be spent to protect your money. Unfortunately, some people out there just don't get it, and those people have to learn their lessons the hard way. That's the bad news. The good news is that I've met a few of those people over the years, and now I can share their stories with you. If you're willing to pay attention to lessons learned by others, you won't have to learn your lessons the hard way.

I wish you could meet my friend Jessica. She's what I call a real survivor. Jessica is one of those kids who, every time they get knocked down, they get right back up and never give up. Jessica has had her share of problems in life; in fact, she has had way more than her share. Jessica has been living on her own since she was 16 years old, moving from one foster home to another, because both of her parents are alcoholics.

When I met Jessica, she was going to high school half a day and then working two jobs after school. She was a bright, responsible girl who worked hard for her money and lived on a budget. Unfortunately, Jessica's budget priorities were a little out of order.

One Friday night after work, Jessica got into her car and drove off to meet some friends at the movies. That night her life would become like a movie – the worst horror movie you can imagine.

One minute, Jessica was heading to the movie theater to meet friends, and the next minute her car was flipping over and over, through a busy intersection, and into on-coming traffic. Some idiot had run a red light and crashed into Jessica's car, knocking her unconscious instantly. Jessica has no memory of the crash, which is lucky for her, because it's not an experience anyone would ever want to recall.

Just getting through each day was going to be challenging enough for Jessica without having to replay the nightmare over and over in her mind.

Jessica remained in a coma for days. When she finally woke up in the hospital, her body was in casts from head to toe. She had broken bones throughout her body, and the pain was so intense that it even hurt to breathe.

Jessica spent several weeks in the hospital and was still unable to walk when they finally sent her home, but she had faced adversity before and was determined to recover from her physical injuries. Over the next year, Jessica dealt with the pain of daily physical therapy, endured several operations, and spent her days in a wheelchair. But her determination paid off as she slowly recovered, learned to walk again, and finally was able to go back to school.

Isn't that a great ending to a horrible story?

It would be, if only that were really the end of the story, but it's not; it's just the beginning. One day after school, Jessica stopped by her mailbox on the way back to her apartment. As she walked up to the mailbox, she was thinking how great it was to be walking again and to be out of that crummy wheelchair. She was definitely getting stronger physically, and life was looking brighter.

Jessica grabbed her mail and headed back to the apartment. The first envelope she opened was from the hospital she had been in for several weeks. Unfortunately, it wasn't exactly a "get well" card. It was more like a "get sick" card.

The envelope in Jessica's hand contained the first of many bills that would find their way into her mailbox over the next few months. This bill was for $52,000!

Jessica felt like someone had just smacked her on the head with a baseball bat. Her stomach was in knots, and she felt like throwing up. The bills kept coming – from doctors, physical therapists, labs, pharmacies, and surgeons. It was $2,000 here and $5,000 there. Before long, Jessica had more than $100,000 in medical bills piled up on her kitchen table – all because some drunk driver ran a red light and plowed into her car one Friday night.

In a perfect world, the drunk driver would have had automobile insurance to cover the cost of Jessica's medical treatment as well as her car that was totaled in the crash. Unfortunately, as you know, this is not a perfect world – that drunk driver had no insurance, he had no money, and he was in jail. Nobody was going to help Jessica pay her bills. At the age of 18, Jessica was in debt to the tune of $100,000.

My friend Jessica had her life turned upside down by this experience. She went to bed scared and stressed out every night for years as she struggled to pay off her debts.

DID YOU KNOW?

40% of all personal bankruptcies are due to medical bills.

...NOW YOU KNOW.

Why did Jessica end up in this horrible situation? The answer to this question is sad, but true. Jessica ended up in the mess she was in because of two decisions she could not have controlled and one decision that she could have controlled.

A man whom Jessica did not know decided *not* to buy automobile insurance, which is against the law. That same man also decided to drive under the influence of alcohol on that Friday night. These two decisions were made by someone else; Jessica had no control over these decisions.

But there was one more decision that Jessica could have controlled, a decision that could have saved her almost $100,000.

Before her accident, Jessica worked at a restaurant that offered health insurance. To get the coverage, Jessica would have had to pay $150 per month – that's $5.00 per day. That's one decent tip from one table at the restaurant where she worked. But Jessica made the decision *not* to buy health insurance, through the restaurant or anywhere else, because she didn't think she could afford it, and she didn't think she would need it. After all, she was only 18, and she didn't plan on getting sick anytime soon.

Jessica could not have been more wrong about this decision, because health insurance is not just for old people or for people who think they will soon be sick. Health insurance is for every living, breathing person.

If Jessica had spent the $150 per month for health insurance at her job, she would have had to pay only about $2,000 of her $100,000 in medical bills. Jessica thought that she could not afford health insurance. The truth is, she could not afford *not to buy* health insurance because as she now knows, bad things can happen to good people, and you cannot control the decisions that other people make. Jessica's decision not to buy health insurance was a $100,000 mistake.

Remember the $150 per month for health insurance Jessica didn't think she could afford? Well now, even if she pays $150 per month towards her $100,000 debt, it will take her more than 50 years to pay it off – and that's without paying interest on that debt. Add to that the monthly cost of health insurance, because you can bet that Jessica will never again walk out of the house without it.

Everybody needs health insurance. This is one of those lessons that you don't have to learn the hard way; my friend Jessica has already learned this lesson for you. There will be things in your budget that you may want to buy, and there will be things in your budget that you must buy. Health insurance is definitely one of the *must buy* items.

When you are no longer on your parents' health insurance, the first dollar you spend should be on a health insurance policy for yourself.

MOVIN' OUT

When? I can't tell you. Where? I don't know. Why? I don't have a clue.

But, what? I'm all over "what."

The "what" is this: someday, somehow, somewhere, just about every one of you is going to move out of your parents' house and get your own place. Chances are, you may even have a roommate. You may move into an apartment, a house, a trailer, or a college dorm. It doesn't matter to me where you end up, because the bottom line is going to be the same.

For 99% of you, the first place you live after you leave your parents will not belong to you. What I'm telling you is that you aren't going to own the first place you live, whether it's a house, an apartment, a trailer, or a dorm. And if *you* don't own it, that means somebody else does. Unless that someone else is your mom or dad or your favorite uncle (and I don't mean Uncle Sam), you aren't going to be living there for free. The bottom line is *you will pay rent.*

There is nothing wrong with paying rent. Almost all people do it at some point in their lives. Since most people don't have enough money to buy a house when they move out on their own for the first time, renting a place to live is very common.

The process of renting a place to live is very simple. First, you find an area where you want to live, and you look for a place that you can afford to rent. Then, you negotiate a price and fill out an application for the person or company that owns the place. If you are renting from a person, he or she is called a landlord. If you are renting from a company, it will be called the lessor or leasing agent. If your credit is good, and it looks and smells like you bathe at least twice a week, you will probably be approved to rent the place.

But, if your credit is not good, you probably won't get to rent the place, and you may end up living with your parents for a lot longer than you had planned. It's not hard to mess up your credit. Write a couple of bad checks, pay your credit card bill late, forget to pay your cell phone bill, and—BAM!—you have bad credit. Nobody wants to rent a place to you, nobody wants to sell a car to you, and you are stuck at your parents' house forever with nothing but your two feet and maybe a bike for transportation.

If you do survive the credit application, the next step in the process is signing a lease. When you sign that lease, you usually are agreeing to do four things:

1. To pay rent every month until the lease is up. This may be six months, one year, or more.

2. To give written notice a certain number of days (30, 45, or 60) before the date you plan to move out. If you don't, you could get stuck with paying more rent on the place even after you move out.

3. To pay your rent on time. You can't pay a week late or even one day late.

4. To take care of the place you are renting. Simply put, it needs to look the same on the day you move out as it did on the day that you moved in.

The landlord or leasing agent is going to make you put down money for a security deposit to cover any damage you or anybody else may do to the place. So taking good care of the place is pretty important. The concept is simple; if you mess the place up, you lose your deposit.

WARNING! If you're going to have roommates, make sure they sign their names on the lease with you. Don't ever sign your name on a lease by yourself if someone else is going to be living with you, even if a roommate moves in with you days, weeks, or months later. Make sure the lease is signed – right then, right there. Don't make any exceptions for anyone, not even for your best friend. And when any roommates move in, make sure they kick in their fair share of the security deposit as well. An argument over money is one of the quickest ways to lose a friend.

After you all sign the lease, pay your deposits, and move your belongings into the place, you will have to make a few choices. Some of these choices are no big deal, like which channels you want with your cable TV package, but other choices you will make could quite possibly ruin your life.

Most people decide where to live based upon how much rent they can afford. That's a good place to start, but it's not the whole story. It's most of the story, but it's never all of the story. After paying rent each month, there are always several more bills to pay when you live on your own. Unless your parents own a grocery store, you will need to buy food—week after week, month after month, year after year—for the rest of your life. It's a simple fact of life; eat or die.

Candles are great, but most people like to turn on the lights every once in a while. So, electricity is usually a necessity, and electricity is not free. Turn on the lights, watch TV, run the air conditioner, and then sit back and wait for the electric bill to arrive. If the place you rent doesn't have gas, your electric bills will grow every time you cook, wash clothes, or run the dishwasher. Whether it's gas or electric, you pay either way.

So, you have to pay for food, electricity, gas, water, and maybe cable television. These are the kinds of bills that you will be faced with every month when you live on your own. If you're lucky, they will all come in at the same time so your state of depression won't last too long. When you rent a place to live, these bills that come in every month are the rest of the story, *almost.*

Why did I say *almost*? What else is there for you to worry about when you rent a place to live?

Listen up! Read the next few pages very carefully, because if you don't, you may make the most expensive mistake of your life.

If you don't believe me, maybe you will believe Angela Gault. I realize that you probably don't know who Angela Gault is, but you don't have to know people to learn from their mistakes.

A few years ago, Angela rented a one-bedroom apartment just outside of Atlanta, Georgia. She lived in that apartment with five roommates: four cats and a dog. Angela's rent was $400 a month. The apartment wasn't very large, so it was stuffed with everything Angela owned at the time – TV's, a stereo, CD's, furniture, and all of her clothes.

Everybody has stuff – some have a lot and some have a little. It doesn't matter how much or how little you have; if you own it, then you don't want to lose it. Every single item that Angela Gault owned was inside her apartment.

Angela's apartment was on the second floor of a two-story building, so she had a clear view of an old building across the street that was falling apart and looking pretty bad. Naturally, Angela and the other tenants in her building were happy when they found out that a developer had bought the old building and started a huge renovation to convert the run-down building into brand-new apartments. Angela was looking forward to the day when the view from her second floor apartment would be really nice. That day never arrived.

On April twelfth, Angela went to work like she did every other Tuesday. A few hours later, her life was ripped apart like a banana in a blender. At 1:15 in the afternoon, Angela's cell phone rang. Before she could even say hello, a shaky voice at the other end of the line told her to get into her car and get back to her apartment as fast as she could. The whole building was on fire!

At that moment, it did not matter how the fire had started. All Angela could think about was her four cats and her dog locked in her apartment on the second floor of the building. How could Angela have known that some absent-minded construction worker across the street would forget to turn off his welding torch when he left for lunch? How could anyone have known that the fire across the street in the old, run-down building would be so big that it would spread across the street to Angela's building? Nobody could have ever predicted that anything like this would happen.

Time out. Make a mental note: *stuff* – stuff that you think will never happen – *happens, and it can happen to you.*

When Angela arrived at the scene of the fire, she couldn't get anywhere near her apartment because the police had set up barricades several blocks away. She couldn't get there, but she could see the flames and smoke coming out of her apartment. The scene was total chaos with firefighters running around and television crews in helicopters covering the five-alarm fire.

Angela was shaking. Her body was numb, and she felt helpless. Angela knew she couldn't stop the fire, but she also knew that when she went to work that morning, she had left four cats and a dog in the same apartment that was burning to the ground. Somehow, the dog and two of her cats managed to escape from the burning building, but the other two cats never made it out of the horrific blaze.

Angela Gault lost everything she owned when her apartment burned to the ground that day. Some of the things she lost were worth a lot of money, and some of what she lost was worth a lot more than money. I asked Angela how much she would have guessed all of her belongings were worth before she had this horrible experience. She said her guess would have been about $25,000.

That was a bad guess. When it was all added up – furniture, clothes, shoes, televisions, a stereo, art, and more than 1,000 CD's – the value of everything Angela owned was more than $50,000.

DID YOU KNOW?

Each year, Americans lose $8.6 billion in personal property that was destroyed by a fire.

...NOW YOU KNOW.

Fortunately, when you rent an apartment, a house, a trailer, or even a dorm room, you can choose to buy something called renter's insurance that will replace things you lose by theft or in a fire like the one in Angela's building. Unfortunately, Angela Gault decided not to buy renter's insurance.

I asked Angela why she didn't buy a renter's insurance policy that would have cost her as little as $40.00 per month, which she could easily afford. She stared at the floor for a few seconds and then looked up at me and said, "I really didn't think it could ever happen to me."

Time out again. Make another mental note: *it can happen to you.*

The week before the fire, Angela Gault wrote several checks to pay her rent, her electric bill, and her cable bill. But it was the one check that Angela did not write – the $40.00 check for renter's insurance – that could have prevented her life from being turned upside-down. For the next several years, Angela Gault suffered horribly from the pain of her losses.

You see, Angela knew about renter's insurance. Someone had told her how important it was to buy renter's insurance, but she still chose not to buy it.

I realize that you don't know Angela Gault, but remember, you don't have to know people to learn from their mistakes. Almost every one of you will rent a place to live in one day. Make sure you buy a renter's insurance policy before you put so much as a toothbrush inside that place.

This was a tragic and expensive lesson for Angela Gault, but it can be a very cheap lesson for you. If you can't afford the renter's insurance policy, you can't afford to rent the place.

Bad stuff happens to good people. Be prepared.

the deal on wheels

No matter where you go, eventually you leave that place and go somewhere else. And when you get somewhere else, you don't stay there forever, either; you might hang out there for a few minutes, a few hours, or even a whole day, but eventually you leave there as well and move on to your next stop. That's just the way life works.

This process starts when you are born and continues your whole life. First you crawl, then you walk, next you run, later you ride a bike, and on and on. So, it's not a matter of *if* you are going to go from place to place, it's simply a matter of *how* you're going to go from place to place – what your means of transportation will be. This is all part of a process leading you up to the top of the *means of transportation* ladder. The top of this ladder is a place most young people think about and talk about for several years until they reach the top.

What does it mean to be at the top of the *means of transportation* ladder? When you reach the top of this ladder, you can decide where you want to go and when you want to go, wherever it is you're going.

You reach the top of the *means of transportation* ladder when you finally buy your very own car. I'm not talking about when somebody gives you a car or when you borrow your parent's car. I'm talking about that day when you walk into that car dealership and sign on the dotted line where it says "owner of vehicle," not co-owner, not friend of the owner, and definitely not son or daughter of the owner. The car is yours – you own it, sort of.

The good news is that this is the top of the ladder – the car you buy belongs to you. The only bad thing is that a lot of people fall off the top of this ladder. It's a long way down, and it can be very painful when you hit the bottom. Most people who fall off the top of the *means of transportation* ladder fall because they forgot to learn some of the secrets about buying and operating a car before they got to the top. They only think about how much their monthly car payment will be, and they forget to consider how much it is going to cost to operate and maintain their vehicle. This is a huge mistake that lots of people make – both smart people and people who aren't so smart.

The FIRM Factor

When you're trying to figure out what size monthly car payment you can afford, make sure you add the FIRM factor to your monthly budget, which stands for <u>f</u>uel, <u>i</u>nsurance, <u>r</u>epairs, and <u>m</u>aintenance. FIRM is an estimate of how much money you will need to cover things like gas, oil changes, regular service, new tires, repairs, and insurance. These things will always cost way more than you think they will cost, so get ready.

Fuel, repairs, and maintenance are a little difficult to estimate. But to figure out how much your car insurance will cost, it just takes one phone call to a local insurance agent or to your parents' agent. If you tell the agent exactly what car you want to buy, you can get an estimate on what your insurance will cost each month. Unlike renter's insurance and health insurance, having car insurance is not an option; it's the law. No insurance, no wheels.

Here's an idea. Whatever your car payment is per month, make sure you can afford at least twice that amount to cover your FIRM. So, if your car payment is $300 per month, be prepared for gas, oil, tires, service, repairs, and insurance to cost you another $300 or more each month over the life of your loan. Your FIRM could easily be that much every month since one major repair can eat up several months' worth of FIRM, so be prepared.

Think of FIRM in the same way as renter's insurance; if you can't afford the renter's insurance policy, then you can't afford the rent. The deal on cars is the same; if you don't think you can afford the FIRM (fuel, insurance, repairs, and maintenance), then you can't afford the vehicle you want to buy.

The Flushing Sound

Most people who buy a car have to borrow money to pay for it. Very few people can walk into a car dealership and pay cash or write a check for the full price of the car they are buying. So, it is not completely true to say that people who borrow to buy a vehicle really "own" their car. It is more accurate to say that they "owe on" their car, which is very different from owning their car. I guess if you said, "owe on" really fast, over and over, it might start to sound like "own," but it just isn't the same, no matter how fast you say it.

When you borrow money to buy a car, you go into debt for something that will definitely be worth a lot less when you sell it than it was worth when you bought it. It's called *depreciation*, and it happens to most stuff you buy including cars, boats, TV's, computers, furniture, and more.

My dad made a rule in our house when I was a kid that said, "Don't buy anything that you can't pay for today, unless what you are buying is going to be worth more tomorrow than it is today." He was talking about just the opposite of depreciation. He was trying to teach us to borrow money only to buy things that would become more valuable over time, like a house or land. This is called *appreciation* – when things get more valuable. This is the exact opposite of *depreciation* – when things get less valuable starting the moment you buy them – like **cars**.

That's right; the minute you drive your car off the dealership lot, it will be worth considerably less than it was worth ten minutes earlier when the salesperson was telling you what a great deal you were getting on the car. This might really make you mad, but the truth is that most new cars depreciate as much as 20% the day you drive them off the lot. That means if you walk into a dealership and Sammy-the-slick-salesman talks you into buying a brand-new $25,000 SUV, the minute you drive off the lot, you might as well flush $5,000 of your hard-earned cash right down the toilet. If you changed your mind the next day and tried to sell your car back to slick Sammy, he would pay you only about $20,000 for the same car you just drove off the lot yesterday. A year later, you can flush again, and you can keep on flushing – to the tune of about 15% each year – until the day you sell your vehicle.

All cars, trucks, and SUV's depreciate, and they depreciate for four reasons: make/model, age, mileage, and condition. The problem with this is that you may have borrowed $15,000 to pay for a new car, but two years later, that same car is worth only $10,000. If you need to sell your car, the most you would get is $10,000, but you would still owe approximately $12,000 on your loan that has to be paid off even if you sell the car. This is called being *upside-down* on a car loan; you owe more money for the car than the car is worth. It usually happens when you get a longer pay-back time, or *term*, on your car loan, like five or six years, to keep your monthly payments lower. Lower is not always better.

Another quick way to get upside-down on your car loan is to put too little money down when you buy a car. If you want a lower monthly car payment, save your money a while longer before you buy, so you can put more money down on the car you choose to buy. Trust me, upside-down is something you never want to be. If you aren't sure you fully understand the concept of upside-down, go stand on your head, upside-down, for 15 minutes. Then, remember that feeling because that's how it's going to feel if you get upside-down on a car loan.

That's why it's so important to know a few minor tricks about buying a vehicle before you reach the top of the *means of transportation* ladder. Depreciation can really sting, no matter how you look at it, but there are a few secrets that can ease the pain of depreciation and even make it work to your advantage.

Here's the secret: buying a brand-new car is a waste of money. When I decide to buy a "new" car, it's never really new. I mean it's "new" to me, but it's not really new – like "brand-new." I always try to buy a vehicle with at least 25,000 miles on it, because that's how you get your best deal and avoid getting upside-down on your car loan. Most depreciation on cars takes place between zero and 25,000 miles, so if you buy a vehicle after 25,000 miles, you get to buy it for way less – at the depreciated cost – and someone else gets to take the financial hit.

There's one more even bigger waste of money than buying a new car: *leasing it*. Most people who lease cars get a vehicle that they really can't afford, and when the lease is up, they have to give the car back to the dealer, so they end up with nothing to show for the money they spent. That means 100% of their money goes right down the toilet – big flush.

DID YOU KNOW?

Nearly 40% of all millionaires choose to buy used cars rather than new ones.

...NOW YOU KNOW.

My dad's rule about not borrowing money to buy anything that depreciates was a good rule then and would be a good rule now, with one exception: automobiles. Ideally, you would save your money for a few years and then buy a used car with cash and have no car payment. However, the reality is that most young people will borrow money to buy their first car. That's just a fact of life, and there's nothing wrong with that.

Tricks of the Trade

A friend of mine used to sell cars for a living. He told me that some car salespeople love to sell cars to young people because it's so easy to confuse them and convince them that they are getting a great deal when, in fact, they are getting a rotten deal. That's because a lot of times young people are so caught up in the excitement of getting a car that they never even bother to do their car-buying homework. And, while homework for school can be the ultimate pain, car-buying homework can put some serious cash in your pocket.

The Internet is a great source for anyone who is thinking about buying a car – new or used. Everything you need to know about buying cars, calculating monthly payments, and checking out interest rates is within a simple click of the mouse.

If you don't have Internet access, go to a library or bookstore and look at these three publications: *Consumer Reports Car Buying Guide* (on the magazine racks), *Edmund's Automobile Buyers Guide*, and *Kelley Blue Book*. The information in each of these books is usually available online for free.

Before you get face to face with someone who wants to sell you a car, you have to do your homework. You need to know four key things:

1. How much you can afford to spend on car payments and FIRM – this amount needs to be built into that monthly budget we talked about earlier.

2. How much the car you want is going to cost – get this information for free at Edmunds.com and KelleyBlueBook.com.

3. Your "auto beacon" credit score from a credit-reporting agency (get it online at MyFico.com, Equifax.com, TransUnion.com, and Experion.com) – so you can find out what interest rate you can expect to qualify for.

4. What your interest rate might be if you get a car loan from a local bank – check out Bankrate.com for interest rates in your area and auto loan calculators to figure out your payments.

If you do this homework, you will be prepared for the process, and you won't get ripped off. Whether you are buying a car from an individual or a slick car salesperson, if you show up armed with information, you will always have a much better experience.

Homework is one thing, but making the deal is a different game altogether. Here's the inside scoop that most car dealers *don't* want you and your friends to know:

1. The best time to get the best deal on a car is the last few months of the year when dealers are trying to get older models (new and used) off the lot. The best time of the month to buy a car is toward the end, because salespeople are motivated to sell certain numbers of vehicles each month. So, they're always willing to make a better deal near the end of the month.

2. The sticker price on the window of a new car is usually a joke. Anybody who pays that price is a real sucker. You should ignore that price and start negotiating at what dealers call their "invoice" price. Try to end up as close to that price as possible.

Here's some free advice for negotiating your best price on a car:

- When you walk into the dealership, negotiate with the salesperson as if you are going to buy a car that day.

- Never buy a car that day.

- Check out several dealerships that sell the make and model vehicle you want.

- Get the dealer's "best" price in writing before you walk out of the place.

- Tell the salesperson you are going to another dealership in town to compare prices.

- If you get a better price, go back to the first dealer and see if they will beat the new price you just got. Make them beat it, not just match it.

- Always, always, make sure the salesperson understands that you are more than willing to walk away from the deal you are being offered.

3. Car dealers make tons of money on financing the cars they sell. Don't ever let a salesperson start the sales pitch by asking you what amount you want your monthly car payment to be. That's the easiest way for them to get you to pay way more for the vehicle than you should. They will always find a way to get you to the monthly payment you want, while at the same time, charge you more for the car than you should pay.

4. Always walk into the dealership and tell the salesperson that you would like to get their best price *without* financing. When you finally agree to consider financing, tell the salesperson what interest rate you expect to get (from your car-buying homework). Make sure the salesperson understands that you will be getting financing prices from other dealers before you make your final decision.

When you consider your monthly car payment, try to get a loan for the shortest period of time possible – four years is good, three years is better, five years is dangerous, and six years is crazy. If you take too long to pay off your car, you will be upside-down on your loan. Remember that upside-down headstand!

DID YOU KNOW?

If you borrow $20,000 to finance a car for 5 years at 12% interest, you will actually end up paying $26,700 for that vehicle.

...NOW YOU KNOW.

This isn't everything you need to know to keep your balance on the top of the *means of transportation* ladder, but it will definitely help. Second only to credit card debt, the cost to finance, insure, repair, and operate a vehicle is the biggest cause of financial disaster for young people in America.

Most adults think young people are clueless when it comes to buying and operating cars. Do me a favor; do your homework, and prove all those old folks wrong. See you on the road.

easy money

Does this headline look familiar?

"Parents of 15-year-old find $71,000 cash hidden in his closet"

It should look familiar. You probably saw this story featured recently on a nightly news program. It was all over the major networks and the newspapers.

I saw the story, and it was unbelievable. The boy's mother was cleaning and putting away laundry when she came across a large, brown paper bag buried beneath some clothes and a skateboard in the back of her 15-year-old son's closet. Nothing could have prepared her for the shock she experienced when she opened the bag and found it was full of cash: five-dollar bills, twenties, fifties, and hundreds – all neatly rubber-banded in labeled piles.

"My first thought was that he had robbed a bank," said the boy's 41-year-old mother. "There was over $71,000 dollars in that bag. I couldn't believe it."

The woman immediately called her husband at the car dealership where he worked to tell him what she had discovered. He came home right away, and they drove together to the boy's school and picked him up. They were in for a huge surprise when they heard where all the money had really come from.

As it turns out, the boy had been sending out a type of e-mail chain letter to addresses that he found on the Internet. Every day after school for the past two months, he had been doing this on his computer in his bedroom.

"I just got the e-mail one day, and I figured, 'What the heck.' I put my name on it like the instructions said, and I started sending it out," said the clever 15-year-old.

The e-mail letter listed three addresses and contained instructions first to send one five-dollar bill to the person at the top of the list, then to delete that address, move the other two addresses up, and finally, to add your name to the bottom of the list. The letter said that if you send the e-mail to ten people (and they each send the message to ten more people, and so on), you will receive several thousand dollars in five-dollar bills within two weeks - if you just send out the e-mail letter with your name at the bottom of the three-person list.

"I get junk e-mail all the time, and I really didn't think it was gonna work," the boy explained, "but it did."

Within the first few days of sending out the e-mail, the post office box that his parents had gotten him for his video-game magazine subscriptions began to fill up not with magazines, but with hundreds of envelopes containing five-dollar bills.

"About a week later I rode my bike down to the post office, and my box had one magazine and about 300 envelopes stuffed inside. There was also a yellow slip that said I had to go up to the (post office) counter. I thought I was in trouble or something," laughed the boy, as he continued explaining. "I went up to the counter, and they had a whole box of more mail for me. I had to ride back home and empty out my backpack 'cause I couldn't carry it all."

Over the next few weeks, the boy continued sending out the e-mail. "The money just kept coming in, and I just kept sorting it and stashing it in the closet. I barely had time for my homework," he laughed. He had also been riding his bike to several of the area's banks and exchanging the five-dollar bills for twenties, fifties, and hundreds.

"I didn't want the banks to get suspicious, so I just kept riding to different banks with, like, five thousand dollars at a time in my backpack. I would usually tell the lady at the bank counter that my dad had sent me in to exchange the money for larger bills, and he was outside waiting for me. One time the lady gave me a really strange look and told me that she wouldn't be able to do it for me, and my dad would have to come in and do it, so I just rode to the next bank down the street, and they did it for me."

Surprisingly, the boy didn't have any reason to be afraid. The news team that first reported the story investigated the so-called "chain letter" the boy was sending out and found that it wasn't a chain letter or a pyramid scheme at all. In fact, it was completely legal according to the U.S. Postal and Lottery Laws, Title 18, Section 1302 and 1341, and Title 18, Section 3005 in the U.S. code, and also in the code of federal regulations, Volume 16, Sections 255 and 436.

Turns out, the 15-year-old boy had made all that $71,000 legally, and it was his to keep. The best part of all is that I can let you in on the secret and explain to you exactly how he made his $71,000, and if you follow my simple directions, you can bank on getting that much money, or even more, for yourself.

If this sounds like a great opportunity to make some easy cash, and you want in on the deal, then I have some news for you: *you just fell for a typical Internet scam.* What you just read is completely untrue, completely made-up, and completely illegal. And the only thing a scam like this will do for you is help you lose your hard-earned money. In fact, you may have already received this e-mail or letter in your mailbox. This scam has been around for a while, and it's usually targeted at young people like you.

Many people are aware that chain mail is illegal, so when they receive one, they forward it to the FTC (Federal Trade Commission) e-mail address for reporting chain letters. That address is uce@ftc.gov. The FTC then contacts all the addresses from the chain letters. They might even pose as a fake name and address to catch the person sending them money or information. If you participate in a chain-mail scam, the FTC can catch you every time.

So, what happens if you get caught participating in an e-mail scam? First, you will have to return all the money you received illegally. From then on, the FTC will watch everything you do on the Internet. Finally, you may have to pay a big fine, and you might even get thrown in jail.

If you don't believe me, ask John Lutheran, Megan Estenson, or Paul Boivin. They are just a few of the latest chain-mail spammers that received a call from the FTC. They all got caught, and they all found themselves in big trouble with the federal government. Trust me, if you're going to get in trouble, get in trouble with your parents, your teacher, or even your boss, but whatever you do, don't get in trouble with the federal government. These guys do not mess around, and they won't hesitate to throw you in jail if you make a habit of getting involved with these scams.

It's pretty simple: if you get a letter in the mail that looks like a "get rich quick" chain letter, please rip it up and throw it in the trash. Likewise, if you get an e-mail that looks suspicious, don't hesitate, and don't even think twice – just left click on "delete." Just remember this: chain mails of any kind that involve money are always illegal, period. No exceptions – not for me, not for you, not for the man on the moon.

How do you recognize chain-mail or pyramid scams?

- They always ask you to send some amount of money – usually $5.00 – to someone you don't know.

- They always promise you'll make a huge amount of money (like $46,000) in a certain number of days.

- They always claim they are legal, and they usually cite some law that says they are. Chain mails involving money are completely illegal.

- They usually include a success story of someone who made a lot of money from a chain mail. These stories are lies to make you believe the chain letter will work.

- They usually say that "this is not considered chain mail by the post office."

Chain-mail scams aren't the only types of scams targeted at young people; they are just one of the thousands of ways that people you don't even know will try to get you to hand over your hard-earned money. Over the years, the stories will change, and the dollar amounts will grow, and they will always tempt you. Here are some popular scams targeted at young people:

1. **You just won!** Someone calls or e-mails or a window pops up on your computer screen to tell you that you've just won an incredible vacation. You only need to give your credit card number to cover the taxes on your "free" vacation, and you're on your way. But, to claim your free trip, you have to book it today! Ignore it. These people are crooks.

2. **Lowest price ever!** Some online auctions and banner ads promise super-low prices for things like popular video games and software. They want you to send cash, a money order, or your bank account information before you ever receive anything. Forget it. They're trying to rip you off.

3. **You're going to be famous!** A commercial says that a casting agency is looking for people of all ages to act in commercials and movies and invites you to a free audition with agents from New York and Los Angeles. At the audition you're told that all you need to do to get started is to spend hundreds – or even thousands – of dollars on photos and acting lessons, but they think that you *really* have what it takes. Laugh at it. It's a total scam.

4. **Make $20 an hour from home!** Signs on the street or flyers near schools advertise easy ways for you to make money. When you call the number, they tell you to just send in $50 to find out how to make the big bucks. Don't fall for it. These scumbags just want your money.

Whether someone tries to scam you on the Internet, on TV or radio, over the phone, or in person, scams usually all have a few things in common. They always tell you that great things will happen to you - that you can be rich, famous, or take free trips - but they also always have an even more important ingredient to beware of. They always ask you to spend your hard-earned money *first* - *before* something great will supposedly happen to you. There's an old saying that says, "There's a sucker born every minute." Don't be one of those suckers.

DID YOU KNOW?

Almost 50% of all Internet scams reported to the FTC were from people who got ripped off through Internet auctions.

...NOW YOU KNOW.

These types of scams are becoming really popular ways to rip off teenagers. They're one more way for criminals to steal from unsuspecting, innocent young people – but it's not the easiest way for crooks to work their dirty tricks.

Scum-of-the-earth criminals will steal from anybody, anytime, and they don't care who gets hurt along the way.

Most of you are going to work really hard to earn your money and, hopefully, you will work equally hard to protect that money. The rotten thing about it is that one day you could be getting ripped off without even knowing that it's happening.

A long time ago before credit cards were common, most people walked around with a pretty good amount of cash in their pockets, wallets, or purses. Strange things happened to a lot of people back then. They would leave their house or apartment for the day with cash in their wallet, and they would not spend any money all day. Then, when they got home that night, they would open their wallets and discover that most, if not all, of their cash was gone – disappeared, *not there*. The same wallet that had money in it in the morning was somehow completely empty that night.

These people were getting robbed, and they didn't even know it was happening. And obviously, they had no idea who had robbed them. That's because they were all victims of what were known as pickpockets – people who carefully, quietly, and quickly slip your wallet right out of your pocket or purse, steal your money, and then put the wallet back, so skillfully that you never even realize it has happened.

Today, there aren't as many scumbag pickpockets running around, probably because people don't carry as much cash these days. Unfortunately, though, the world will always have its share of crooks and con-artists, and a lot of times these criminals are people you would least expect to be rotten. In fact, in many cases, the person that cleans out your wallet is someone you already know.

It happened to Shilo Puckett, and it could easily happen to you.

Shilo Puckett grew up in Ohio and spent the first nine years of her life doing all the things that most kids do – playing at the park, swimming during the summer, hanging out with friends, and watching TV at home. Just a few months after her ninth birthday, however, Shilo's life was torn apart.

The police were looking for Shilo and planned to arrest her as soon as they found her. Shilo was only in the third grade, and the charges against her were enough to put her in jail for a long, long time. No one could believe that this sweet little girl could be in any kind of trouble, but, apparently, she was in really big trouble.

When all the facts of the case were sorted out, the evidence showed that Shilo Puckett had been charging purchases on her credit cards all over town for several years and had never paid any of her bills. In fact, Shilo had charged more than $14,000 on 17 different credit cards that were issued in her name – all this from a little girl who was only *nine years old*!

Everyone in town was in shock. Nobody could believe that this nine-year-old could manage to pull off such a stunt. Finally, after several days, there was a break in the case, and the news got better for Shilo, but only temporarily. The police ultimately figured out that Shilo was not the one who actually had spent the $14,000.

Shilo was a victim of identity theft, just like almost ten million other people last year alone. Some low-life crook had stolen Shilo's Social Security number when she was just a toddler and had used that Social Security number to get 17 credit cards in Shilo's name. Then, the crook ran up huge bills on the credit cards and never paid a single credit card bill. In the meantime, Shilo's credit record and financial reputation were being destroyed.

What Shilo went through happens to people every day. Identity theft is like an epidemic. It happens to young people, older people, rich and poor people. It could even happen to you.

DID YOU KNOW?

27 million people have had their identity stolen during the past 5 years.

Nearly 7 million of those people knew the person who stole their identity.

...NOW YOU KNOW.

Since the police finally figured out that Shilo wasn't the crook that they had thought she was, she didn't have to go to jail, but she will have to spend the next several years of her life trying to clear her name, her credit report, and her reputation. That will be almost as miserable as jail itself. Sometimes when your identity is stolen, you're never finished dealing with the financial problems that it causes.

How sick is this? The police finally caught the person who had stolen Shilo Puckett's identity and charged $14,000 on 17 credit cards in Shilo's name. The guilty person was actually a lady that Shilo knew very well – a lady whom she trusted. That lady was sent to jail for six months. Like I said earlier, many people who steal the identity of someone else often steal the identity of someone they know.

Now, I'm not suggesting that your best friend is going to steal your identity, but I am telling you that you have to be extra careful in this day of high-tech transactions. Never give your

Social Security number to anyone unless it is absolutely necessary, and check with your parents before you ever give the number out. Don't ever leave your driver's license out where people can see it. And if you have a birth certificate, keep it hidden so that no one else can find it. These documents are all an identity thief needs to apply for a credit card in your name and ruin your life.

Identity thieves have replaced the pickpockets of the past. Pickpockets used to just steal other people's money. Identity thieves will steal your money and your financial reputation. Your money and your reputation belong to you, so it's up to you and only you to do whatever you have to do to protect them.

Be careful – be smart – especially on the Internet. Bad people do bad things to good people like you.

Final Thoughts

your money, your life

This may be the last chapter in this book, but for you, it's just the beginning of your financial journey.

You may have been surprised to find out that you will earn more than a million dollars during your lifetime. At the same time, you were probably a little annoyed to learn that you'll have to fork over at least 25% of that money to Uncle Sam and his multiple buckets.

You discovered that working part-time as a teen puts you in the same league as some of the most successful people in the world. Once you have a job and money to spend, knowing the difference between needs and wants and being responsible with credit are the best ways to avoid financial disaster.

And, while starting to save early in life and learning to make money while you sleep will both help you get way ahead financially, it should be clear that one of the most rewarding things you can experience is the satisfaction of giving money away to others who are less fortunate than you.

All of the smart things you can do to earn, save, and invest your money are just a big waste of time if you don't manage that money well with a budget and protect yourself with insurance from the bad things that can happen to good people like you.

When it comes to major purchases, like your first vehicle, doing a little homework and knowing the tricks of the trade can help you get the most for your money. And in today's high-tech world, you have to beware and be wise, because there are a lot of low-life crooks out there who will try to rip you off every chance they get. Remember, it's your million dollars, so what you do with it is up to you.

So, there you have it. We know you're going to make money, but we really don't know exactly how much you will make. We know you're going to have to manage your money, but we don't know how well you will manage it. We expect you to multiply your money, but we don't know to what extent you will succeed. And finally, we hope you will protect your money, but we don't know for sure if you will decide to do that or not.

We don't know much, do we? When it comes to money, it's hard to know all the answers, and it's impossible to predict the future.

People who have good-paying jobs sometimes lose their jobs. Low inflation this year could skyrocket next year. Interest rates that are low today might be high tomorrow. An economy that is good can quickly take a dive.

On the flip side, you could get a huge raise next year, the economy could get stronger, interest rates could fall, and the rate of inflation could drop. You might even inherit $100,000 from some distant aunt you haven't seen in ten years. You just never know.

You don't know. I don't know. Nobody knows exactly what the future of your finances will be. But one thing is for sure: your money is *your* money, and what you do with your money is *your* business.

Quite frankly, I don't really care how much money you end up with when you eventually reach your financial destination. I'm a lot more interested in the quality of your journey than I am in your destination. Because one thing I can guarantee you – if you don't enjoy your journey, it's very unlikely that you will enjoy your financial destination.

Here's my point. If you end up with a lot of money, but you are miserable for 40 years while you try to make, manage, multiply, and protect that money, it isn't worth it. The great news is you can have both. You can end up with lots of money, and you can enjoy the ride along the way.

First I'll tell you what doesn't work, and then I'll tell you what does work on the road to financial success.

A lot of adults give young people bad advice when it comes to money and their financial future. They get too wrapped up in the destination and forget to teach young people how to enjoy the journey.

Here's the *wrong* way to approach your financial future. First, think about all the material things you want to have when you get older. Dream about how big you want your house to be. Make a list of all the expensive toys you think you will need. Decide what kind of car, or cars, you want to own later in life. Plan in your mind exactly what kind of lifestyle you see yourself living when you get older.

Next, calculate how much all that stuff is going to cost, including inflation. Estimate how much your monthly bills would be if you lived the lifestyle you are expecting. Then, figure out how much money you will have to earn before taxes so that your take-home pay will cover your living expenses. Now, look in a book or online at a list of careers that would enable you to earn enough money to support your desired lifestyle. Finally, pick one of those careers. Go ahead; choose a career that will pay you enough money to support the lifestyle you think you want.

This is called a *lifestyle-driven journey*. This is also called the biggest mistake you could ever make on the road to financial success. It's backwards, it's wrong, and it is the one thing that most miserable rich people have in common.

They choose jobs for the wrong reasons. They pick their lifestyle first and then try to make their career journey match up with their financial desires, even if their career journey is going to be a horrible one. Most of the time, these people spend their entire journey chasing a lifestyle that is unrealistic. This is the wrong road to financial success, and you don't have to go down that painful, dead-end road.

When I wrote my first book, I concluded that there are four ways to make money – earn it, marry it, steal it, or inherit it. I also concluded that 99% of you will probably have to earn it. That means that just about every one of you will have to work at one or more careers from the time you finish school until the day you retire.

Most people have to work for approximately 86,000 hours before they retire. And, the majority of those people change careers, not just jobs, several times along the way. Hard to believe, but it's true. I'm on my eighth career right now, and I have enjoyed all of them. Eighty-six thousand hours is a long time, so there's nothing wrong with having more than one career during that time.

Those 86,000 hours are the bulk of your financial journey. That's the amount of time you will spend making, managing, multiplying, and protecting your money. And while the road to financial success is always going to have a few bumps along the way, it doesn't have to be a dead-end road. You can make it to your financial destination, and you can still enjoy the journey. Here's how you do it.

First of all, forget about stuff for now. Forget about houses, forget about cars, and forget about vacations. Forget about all the things you can buy with the money you plan to earn, just for a few minutes. I know, you probably think I'm nuts right about now, but just hang in there with me for a little while longer.

The only way to know how it feels to be rich and miserable is to actually *be* rich and miserable. I suspect most of you have not experienced that feeling. Neither have I, but I happen to know a whole bunch of people who have experienced that feeling of having lots of money, huge houses, several cars, and tons of stuff, but they still wake up every day totally miserable and unhappy. I know this is hard for you to imagine, but this is one of those times I'm just going to ask you to trust me. I know lots of people like this, and you probably do, too; they drink too much, they do drugs, they get divorced, they neglect their kids, and sometimes they even commit suicide. That is their dead-end road. They chose it, and they have to live it. You don't.

You can make a better choice. You can make a decision right now, while you are still young, to think about how you will earn your money. What are you passionate about? In what areas do you have natural talents? What kinds of careers interest you? What careers have you tried?

Here's the secret to financial success and satisfaction. First, answer those four questions I just asked. Then, based on your answers to these questions, pursue a career that matches your answers. I don't care what the career is, and I don't care how much it pays. Choosing a career you enjoy is step one to financial success and satisfaction. Remember, it's going to last 86,000 hours. Next, based on the career you choose that matches your passion, your talents, your interests, and your experiences, develop a financial lifestyle that fits the amount of money you will earn in your chosen career.

This is called a *journey-driven lifestyle*. It is the complete opposite of a *lifestyle-driven journey*. A *journey-driven lifestyle* is the secret to financial success and satisfaction.

As I said earlier, I don't care what career you choose because, in the end, it really doesn't matter. If you spend the next 86,000 hours of your life doing something you enjoy, something you are good at, and something that makes the most of your natural talents, then I can assure you, the money will follow.

And that, my young friends, is the absolute bottom line of financial success and satisfaction. The money should *always* follow – the money should *never* lead.

It is much more important for you to be happy than it is for you to be rich. Hopefully, now you understand how you can be both.

Good luck and safe travels on your financial journey.

the bottom lines

Just about every message in life has a bottom line. When it comes to financial literacy – making, managing, multiplying, and protecting your money – there are several bottom lines. It's your money so it's up to you, but here are a few things I've learned about almost all financially successful people.

Financially Successful People:

1. Worked part-time as teenagers

2. Have a career that they enjoy

3. Understand the difference between needs and wants

4. Learned how to save money at an early age

5. Understand how to make money while they sleep

6. Developed good spending habits before they had big bucks

7. Pay the total balance of their credit card bills every month

8. Protect what they own with insurance

9. Realize that there are no real "get rich quick" schemes

10. Recognize the need to live within their means on a budget

11. Give away money to people in need

Financial Stuff

This is a list of financial information that you need to have. If you have this information handy, you will save yourself a lot of time, heartache, and money. Feel free to add to the list.

This is valuable information to have when you need it and dangerous information to lose. Make your list on a seperate piece of paper and give it to one of your parents. DO NOT WRITE YOUR INFORMATION IN THIS BOOK.

1. Social Security #
2. Driver's License #
3. Credit Card Account #'s
4. Credit Card Company Phone #'s (if card is lost/stolen)
5. Auto Insurance Company Name and Policy #
6. Auto Insurance Company Phone # (in case of accident)
7. Auto License Plate # (in case auto is stolen)
8. Renter's Insurance Company Name and Policy #
9. Renter's Insurance Company Phone #
10. Health Insurance Company Name and Policy #
11. Health Insurance Company Phone # (in case of emergency)
12. Automobile VIN # (inside front left door of auto)
13. Auto Car Key # (in case keys are lost or stolen)
14. Computer Passwords
15. Bank Name and Phone #
16. ATM Card # and PIN #
17. Checking Account #
18. Savings Account #
19. Cell Phone Company Name and Phone #

one last thank you

From the minute I started working on this book, I had the unwavering support of many friends and family members. The three people who have paid the greatest price in terms of the time I needed to finish this project are my wonderful wife, Paige, and our precious sons, Graham and Mason. I am so thankful to all of them for their support, patience, and love. I am also grateful to my colleague, Peggy Sandy, for her valuable assistance with the project. Finally, I am thankful to God for the many blessings He has sent my way.

– **Chad Foster**

this book was read by:

name	start date	finish date
1. _____	_____	_____
2. _____	_____	_____
3. _____	_____	_____
4. _____	_____	_____
5. _____	_____	_____
6. _____	_____	_____
7. _____	_____	_____
8. _____	_____	_____
9. _____	_____	_____
10. _____	_____	_____